BASICS OF

TATTOOING

– Learn to tattoo –

OSCAR INFESTAS MARTÍN

Editing, proofreading:	Mentorium GmbH
Editing & cover design:	Oscar Infestas Martín
Layout:	Ayesha Siddique
Photos:	Oscar Infestas Martín, Shutterstock
Production & Publishing:	Amazon KDP

For my wife Alisa and daughters Amelia,
Elena, Nerea and Aaliyah.

You are the most wonderful people.
I love you more than anything.

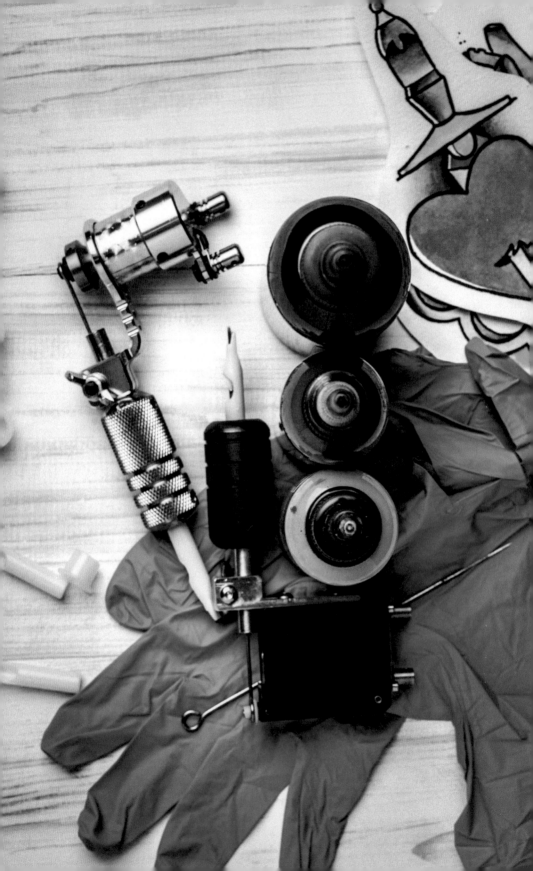

Table of contents

Foreword

My name is Oscar Infestas Martín and I was born in Schwetzingen (Germany) in 1990. Even as a child, I was passionate about the art of drawing. While my siblings played outside, I preferred to live out my creativity and spent several hours a day painting in my nursery. After I got tattooed later in life, I had the idea of trying my hand at the art of tattooing myself. So I quickly ordered a tattoo machine set and started tattooing. My results were disastrous - shaky lines, wrong depths, I didn't even know how to hold the tattoo machine properly. I didn't know anyone who could have taught me how to tattoo. I couldn't afford seminars and there were no non-fiction books on the subject. I was desperate, quickly lost interest and stopped tattooing.

A few years later, I tried again. Now I had the money I needed for seminars, which I attended. From then on, I really enjoyed tattooing because I was getting better and better results and my lines no longer looked like a jagged saw blade. Tattooing became my passion and over the years I was able to gain a lot of knowledge and experience, which I would like to pass on with this book.

Give everything, but never give up."

▪ What you will learn

In this book you will learn all the important basics about tattooing. With the help of pictures, graphics and training plans, both theoretical and practical knowledge is imparted. From setting up different tattoo machines to the finished tattoo - after reading this book and implementing the training plans, you will be able to confidently apply and implement the basics of tattooing you have learned. This book also serves as a guide during the learning process.

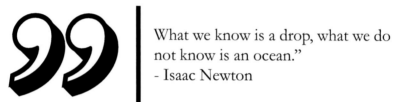

What we know is a drop, what we do not know is an ocean."
- Isaac Newton

▪ Who can learn to tattoo?

You may have asked yourself whether you can learn to tattoo at all. I can tell you that anyone can learn to tattoo, even if they have no previous knowledge of drawing or anything similar. The only thing you need is motivation and a passion for tattooing.

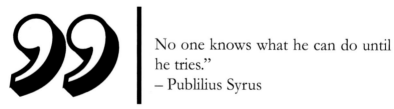

No one knows what he can do until he tries."
– Publilius Syrus

▪ Why this book?

Not everyone has the opportunity to complete an apprenticeship at a tattoo studio or take part in expensive seminars. Many tattoo artists are also reluctant to share their knowledge. In my opinion, we were all born unaware and have learned from other people. So I think that our knowledge is not our property. I decided to write this book to enable new tattoo artists to enter the tattoo world and to pass on my knowledge and experience as a tattoo artist with great pleasure. I wish you lots of fun and success with the following lessons.

Helping one person may not change the whole world, but it can change the world for that one person."

Kind regards

Oscar Infestas Martín

My What is a tattoo?

Tattoos are made up of motifs or texts that are applied under the skin using needles and ink. A tattoo remains permanently under the skin and can only be removed with the help of a laser.

▪ Origin and development

It can be assumed that every ethnic group on earth has both known and practiced tattooing at some point in its development and that it has developed differently from region to region. However, it is disputed in which region the art of tattooing was mainly practiced. The oldest evidence for the occurrence of tattoos comes from Europe. Over 5,000 years ago, the glacier mummy Ötzi bore several charcoal marks that were applied under the skin with needles. These finds can therefore be described as the oldest known tattoos.

Tattoo styles

Which style is preferred is a matter of taste. Because as different as we all are, our preferences are just as different. I will list and explain the most common tattoo styles.

- **Old School / Traditional**

In both cases - whether old school or traditional - we are talking about the seafaring tattoos that were fashionable between 1920 and 1960. They are usually quite colorful, without finely detailed shading. The main feature of old school tattoos is the bold lines of the motif outlines.

- **New School**

The new school style is tattooed in the same way as the old school style, but with young, modern motifs, for example a high heel, cherries etc.

OLD SCHOOL / TRADITIONAL   NEW SCHOOL

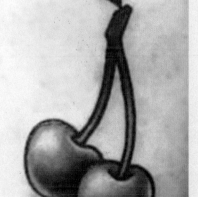

- **Fine Line**

The term fine line refers to tattoos that consist of very delicate and fine lines. These are often very minimalist and small or particularly detailed. Lines that are engraved too finely can partially disappear or fade over time. The disadvantage of such tattoos is that the lines - as with any tattoo - tend to blur. Due to the ageing process of the skin, the lines often run together if this was not taken into account when the tattoo was applied.

- **Dotwork**

Dotworks, so-called dot tattoos, consist of hundreds of tiny tattoo dots that together form a tattoo.

FINE LINE   DOTWORK

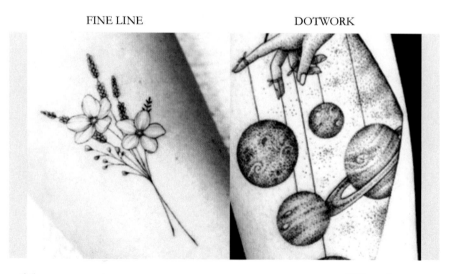

What is a tattoo

- **Blackwork**

Blackwork tattoos are exclusively engraved with black ink. The motifs are diverse - from geometric figures to mandalas and more. The variety of possible designs is endless.

- **Fonts / Lettering**

A very popular tattoo motif is writing as a letter, word, whole sentence or even as longer text. A word is often placed in a banner or is part of another motif.

BLACKWORK   FONTS / LETTERING

What is a tattoo

- **Comic**

A comic tattoo is usually a fun tattoo without any deep meaning. These are colorful designs and cheerful motifs ranging from Marvel characters to Mickey Mouse.

- **Realism**

This includes photorealistic tattoos such as portraits, animal motifs, etc.

COMIC   REALISM

What is a tattoo

- **Watercolour/Aquarell**

Just as on paper or canvas with their dynamic variety of colors, unique works of art are also created on the skin, the diversity of which is virtually unlimited.

- **Sketchy**

Sketchy tattoos are tattoos that resemble a technical pencil sketch. The motif usually looks like an unfinished design. Lines that appear imperfect and unfinished or are hatched in areas. This style is often combined with the watercolor style.

WATERCOLOUR / AQUARELL   SKETCHY

- **Linework**

A tattoo that consists of a line belongs to linework. Motifs of any shape are created from a long line whose curves form an image.

- **Mandala**

Mandalas are generally arranged in a circle and contain constantly repeating patterns. Their multiple changeability makes them so timeless. Often combined with dotwork, mandalas thrive on their symmetry.

LINEWORK   MANDALA

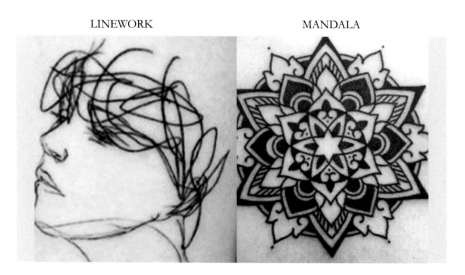

What is a tattoo

- **Asian**

The main motifs for an Asian or Japanese tattoo are dragons, koi carp, geishas, lotus flowers, hanya masks, samurai, etc. Such motifs are usually tattooed against a background of clouds and waves.

- **Maori**

Maori tattoos originated from various Maori Indian traditions. Among the indigenous people of New Zealand, tattoos were part of tribal rituals that displayed a kind of code containing statements about the wearer's origin and rank. Today they belong to a subgroup of the tribals.

ASIAN   MAORI

What is a tattoo

- **Fantasy**

Typical fantasy tattoo motifs include elves, unicorns, dragons, wizards, witches, goblins, warriors, monsters, mythical creatures and Disney characters. The motifs are tattooed in a wide range of variations.

- **Biomechanic**

Biomechanical tattoos differ significantly from conventional tattoo designs such as animals, flowers, dream catchers, etc. Typical of biomechanical tattoos is the open, torn skin, under which not only muscles and bones but also various machine parts such as gears, screws, cables, tubes, hoses, etc. lie. To make the tattoos look realistic, tattoo artists use different colors, shades and techniques.

FANTASY   BIOMECHANIC

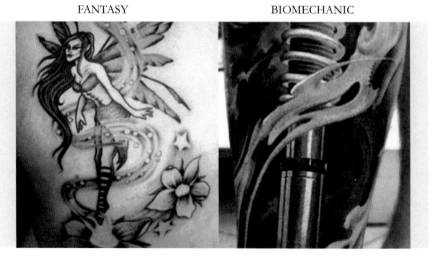

- **Trash Polka**

Trash Polka is also known as Realistic Trash Polka or Buena Vista. This is a young tattoo style that contains realistic and minimalist elements. The most commonly used colors are black, grey and red. Photo-like portraits and motifs are combined with lettering, dots and splashes of color. These tattoos or images create a great visual tension.

- **Black & Grey**

Black & Grey is originally a motif made from black ink. The tattoo artist dilutes the black ink with distilled water, resulting in a lighter shade. Some tattoo artists mix white and black ink to achieve the same result, but this process is rarely used. The Black & Grey tattoos originated in prisons because there were no possibilities to dye tattoos there.

TRASH POLKA BLACK & GREY

What is a tattoo

- **Chicano**

Chicano motifs are usually tattooed in the realistic Black & Grey style. The symbols are mainly women with sombrero and clown faces, weapons, masks, vintage cars, Chicano writings, La Catrinas or skulls.

Cover-up

A cover-up generally refers to a tattoo over a tattoo. An old tattoo is therefore covered over with a new tattoo. An existing tattoo is cleverly incorporated into the new tattoo and ultimately covered up. There are many reasons for a cover-up: a badly done tattoo, spontaneous reasons such as fashion trends and proof of love or a desire to get a tattoo under the influence of alcohol. A cover-up is not easy to create, as numerous factors play a role. These include, for example, the size of the old tattoo, the colors of the old tattoo, the depth of the old tattoo or the new motif desired for the cover-up. Not every motif is suitable for a cover-up and the colors of the existing tattoo provide further specifications. Very dark tattoos in particular can make a cover-up almost impossible. In general, a cover-up is designed like a normal tattoo, with an old tattoo being hidden under a new motif. There are three options for cover-ups:

- **Touching up**

This option is usually used for old, faded tattoos. And, of course, if the customer still likes the old design.

- **Covering**

This involves covering an old tattoo with a new design. In this way lettering or portrait disappears behind a rose or other desired motif.

- **Integrating**

Sometimes it is also possible to integrate the new motif. Humorous tattoo motifs are best suited for this. Of course, it is important that the customer has a good sense of humor and can live with the fact that the failed tattoo is still visible without being the focus of the tattoo.

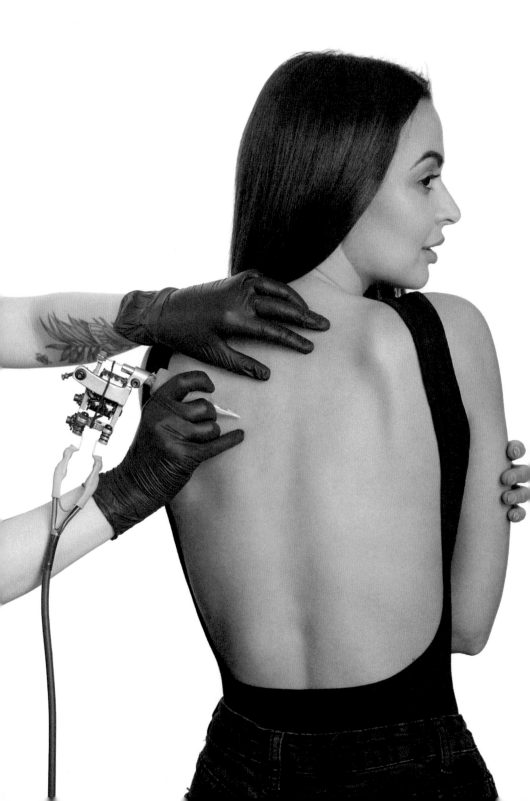

Conditions of the skin

- **Birthmarks**

Birthmarks must not be tattooed. They can be an indicator of malignant changes in the skin, such as skin cancer, and should therefore not be covered with color, as this will make future examinations by the dermatologist more difficult. In such cases, tattoos are usually applied around the birthmark.

- **Stretch marks**

Stretch marks are usually caused by stretching of the skin tissue. They mainly occur after pregnancies and weight gain. It is generally possible to cover stretch marks with a tattoo.

- **Freckles/age spots**

The tattooing of freckles - like the tattooing of age spots - is possible without restriction. However, it should be noted at the design stage that freckles can change and become darker when exposed to sunlight. It is therefore advisable to have the tattoo done when the freckles are at their darkest.

- **Scars/burnt skin**

It is possible to tattoo over a scar or burnt areas of skin, but the wound should be completely healed. The longer it has healed, the better.

- **Pimples**

Pus-filled pimples are inflammations of the skin. You should not get a tattoo on these areas. Remember that this can worsen the inflammation or even cause scarring. As soon as the skin area is free of pimples, nothing stands in the way of getting a tattoo.

- **Neurodermatitis/psoriasis**

I would generally advise against tattoos for skin conditions such as neurodermatitis or psoriasis, as the risk of complications is too high.

- **Poorly healing skin areas**

Areas of skin that heal poorly include elbows, hands, wrists, feet, ankles and knees. These areas of the body are moved a lot in everyday life, which makes healing more difficult. Tattoos on joints tend to heal worse than others and fade much faster. It is usually necessary to re-tattoo these areas several times.

- **Areas of the body that are difficult to tattoo**

Some areas of the body are tighter than others. For example, it is easier to draw a line on a taut area of the body than on a flabby and flexible area of skin. If you are new to tattooing, you should avoid areas of the body that are difficult to tattoo for the time being. You will quickly realize how difficult it is to tighten a soft belly and the needle will not do what you want it to do. The following body regions can be categorized as follows:

- **Areas of the body that are difficult to tattoo**
Belly, neck, inside of upper arm

- **Body parts that are easy to tattoo**
Forearm, back, upper arm

- **Pain during tattooing**
How much pain a tattoo causes depends on the person's perception of pain, the needle grouping used and the body part selected. Contour lines can be compared to lightly scratching the skin. Large needles used to fill areas and for shading tend to feel hot and stinging. Therefore, always be sensitive to your client and always give them the opportunity to take breaks. The following body regions can be categorized as follows in terms of pain sensation:

- **Intense pain**
Ribs, stomach, foot, hand, fingers, neck

- **Medium pain**
Inner upper arm, elbow, neck, chest, thigh

- **Mild pain**
Forearm, calf, back

Tattoo colors

In some countries, there are regulations governing the ingredients of paints. Some substances may not exceed a certain value in order to protect the health of consumers. Check whether and which regulations or provisions apply in your country before purchasing the paint. Only buy high-quality ink so that your engraved work does not suffer from defective ink or even endanger your customer. You will need to find out individually which ink manufacturer you choose, as each ink achieves a different result and can be processed differently. Never store your paints near a heater, as they dry out very quickly due to the heat. The paints must always be shaken well before use. When opening the ink, you should always note the opening date on the ink bottle, as all tattoo inks only have a shelf life of one year after opening. For unopened bottles, follow the expiry date marked on the bottle. With some manufacturers, a protective cap or protective film must always be removed from the ink bottle before using the ink for the first time. Always remember to wear disposable gloves when removing the protective cap so that the paint is not contaminated by your hands. The paint bottles are available in different sizes. Due to the shelf life of an opened bottle of one year, the purchase of a small bottle is often sufficient.

- **Line colors and fill colors**

Many paint manufacturers offer different shades of black, including for lining and filling areas. The so-called "lining black" (used for drawing lines) contains fewer color pigments and therefore does not tend to blow out as quickly as the so-called "filling black". You should therefore not use filling black to draw lines and vice versa.

- **Grey Wash**

Greywash shades consist of black paint diluted with water. Greywash sets contain different dilutions, from dark to soft light gray in different shades. Bear in mind that when applying greywash colors, the reddening of the skin caused by the application process will initially distort the effect of the tones, i.e. the colors will appear much darker when applied than later after the healing process. As a rule of thumb, colors such as black and grey lighten by approx. 30% after healing. Greywash colors can also be mixed by yourself. The following example serves as a guide: Place four color caps on your work table. Fill the first color cap completely with black paint. Fill the second paint cap with six drops of black paint and then distilled water up to the rim. Fill the third paint cap with four drops of black paint and distilled water up to the edge and fill the fourth paint cap with two drops of black paint and distilled water up to the edge. All the paint caps must then be stirred thoroughly so that the paint mixes well with the distilled water. You can always proceed according to this principle, whereby you can adjust the mixing ratio to suit your requirements. However, I recommend buying the Greywash as a ready-to-use product, as this means that the mixing ratio is always the same and it is easier to estimate what the color will look like once it has healed.

▪ Color shades

There are different shades in different consistencies from different manufacturers. Some colors are darker than others when healed. In this case too, you should try out different manufacturers to decide which colors are right for you. As buying an entire range of colors is very expensive, it is possible to buy only the basic colors for the time being and mix them to obtain additional colors. The following color wheel according to Johannes Itten will help you with this.

▪ Color wheel

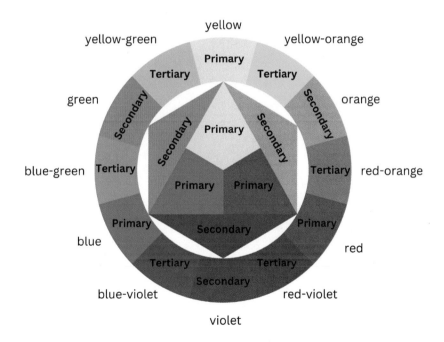

- **Color wheel**

The three primary colors red, yellow and blue can be seen in the middle of the color wheel. They form a triangle and are also called primary colors. There are three further triangles on each of the long sides. Their colors result from the mixture 1:1 of the primary colors below, the so-called secondary colors.

- Red + yellow = orange
- Blue + red = violet
- Yellow + blue = green

Now transfer each color at the tip of the respective triangle to the outer circle and place the 1:1 mixed colors in between - the result is the tertiary colors.

- Yellow + green = yellow-green
- Blue + violet = blue-violet
- and so on.

As you can see, the color wheel is a helpful tool for visualizing the mixing values of colors.

- **Vegan tattoo ink**

Vegan tattoo ink is produced without the use of raw materials of animal origin. Non-vegan ingredients in tattoo inks can be, for example, pigments made from lacquer shield lice, bone charcoal or wool wax.

Stitch depth / skin anatomy

The penetration depth is the extent to which a tattoo needle penetrates the skin with each machine stroke. The depth of the tattoo remains the same on the skin of the entire body. It doesn't matter whether there is a lot of flesh under the skin in a calf tattoo, for example, or whether there are bones just under the skin in a finger tattoo. The depth of the engraving is very important to ensure that the design is engraved cleanly into the skin. It is approx. 1.5 millimeters. The color pigments are inserted through the top layer of skin (epidermis) into the dermis underneath. The color pigments are then deposited in the dermis for the long term.

1. Epidermis
2. Dermis
3. Subcutis
4. Hair

5. Blood vessels
6. Nervs
7. Needle
8. Color pigments

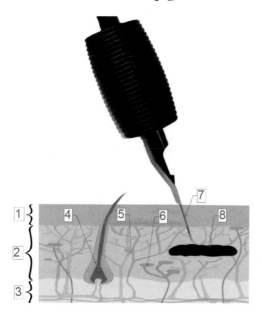

- ## Consequences of too flat engraving

If the tattoo is engraved too shallowly, i.e. only up to the top layer of skin, the tattoo fades considerably or disappears after healing due to rapid skin cell renewal. Flat lines can be recognized by their brownish appearance.

- ## Healing process of the skin

The skin usually begins the peeling process three to four days after the tattoo. When the epidermis loosens, the dead skin becomes white and cracked. It then peels off and the new, healthy skin remains.

FLAT STING   HEALING PROCESS

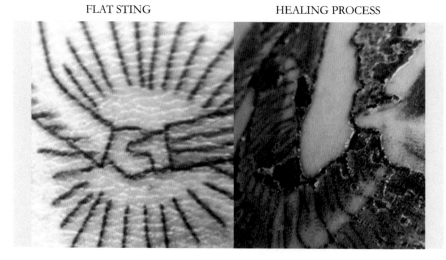

Stitch depth / skin anatomy

▪ Consequences of too deep piercing

If the stitching is too deep, the color reaches a layer of the skin in which the color is no longer trapped, but runs uncontrolled. This leads to unwanted and unsightly shadows around the edges (blow-out). A blow-out cannot be reversed. Stitching too deeply can also cause visible and palpable scarring. Therefore, always be careful and, as a beginner, it is better to stitch too shallowly than too deeply, as a line that is stitched too shallowly can be traced. Over time, you will develop a feel for the right stitch depth.

BLOW-OUT   SCARRING

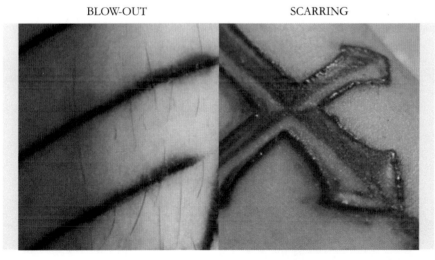

Stitch depth / skin anatomy

Needleology

Tattoo needles usually consist of a grouping of many individual needles. By dipping the needles into the ink, the color adheres between and to the needles thanks to the capillary effect and is applied to the skin through the speed of movement. The right choice of needle can be decisive for the quality of the tattoo, which is why I will introduce you to the different types of needles and areas of application. When buying needles - whether needle bar or needle module - you should always make sure that the needles are of good quality. Cheap needles are often blunt and would injure the customer's skin. The needles themselves are always disposable products that must be properly disposed of in the needle disposal container after use. Never use the same needle on different customers, as there is a risk of transmitting infectious diseases. Needles are always purchased in sterile packaging with an expiry date.

- **Bar needles**

Bar needles are the classic tattoo needles, which are usually used with coil machines. These used to be soldered together by tattoo artists themselves. Nowadays, they can be purchased ready soldered in shops.

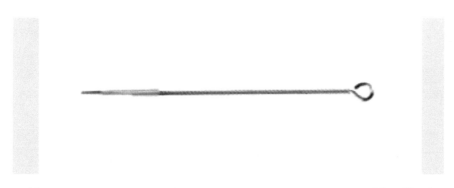

- **Needle modules**

Needle modules are a short needle that is permanently installed in a plastic housing that has the shape of a tip at the front. These are mainly used for rotary machines. The needle module can be inserted into and removed from the handle using a handle. A membrane is built into the housing of the needle module to prevent liquids such as paint, blood or wound fluid from entering the handle. This makes needle modules more hygienic than bar needles.

Needle groupings

▪ Round Liner (RL)

Use: Outer lines/contours (outlines). Needles arranged in a circle with a conical (pointed) tip at the front. The conical taper is achieved by slightly pressing the tips together and soldering them almost to the tip. The distance from the tip to the start of the soldering is only approx. 3 - 5 mm. Needle groups with 3 to 20 needles are commonly used. Some manufacturers also offer single needles, a liner that only consists of a single needle.

▪ Round Shader (RS)

Use: Smaller shading and filling work. Needles arranged in a circle that are soldered together from the upper end. Approx. 10 - 14 mm from the tip to the start of the solder. The needles run straight and a lot of paint can be absorbed in the gaps due to the capillary effect. These needle groups with 3 to 20 needles are commonly used.

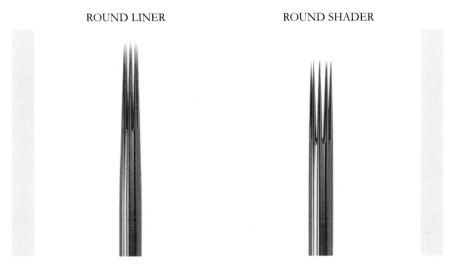

ROUND LINER   ROUND SHADER

Needleology

- **Soft Edge Magnum (SEM) or Round Magnum (RM)**
Use: Shading, filling, coloring. Round Magnum needles are Magnum needles with the needles set back to the outside. This means that the needle points are not in a row as with a magnum, but in a slightly rounded arrangement. These needles ensure that there are no sharp edges when shading and that the image is more even. The skin is therefore less damaged at the edges than with normal magnums. These needle groups with 5 to 15 needles are commonly used.

- **Magnum (M1)**
Use: Filling and shading. Magnum needles are spread flat needles. This means that the needles form two rows at the tip - an odd number of needles in the bottom row and an even number of needles in the top row. The soldering point usually starts 10 - 12 mm from the tip of the needle. The usual sizes for magnum needles are 5 to 15 needles, but there are also much larger sizes with up to 39 and 45 needles.

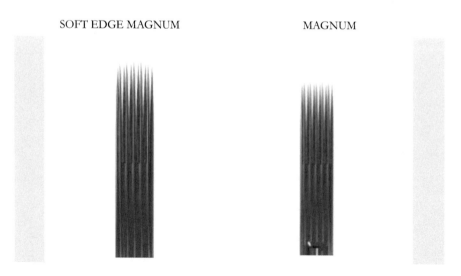

SOFT EDGE MAGNUM   MAGNUM

▪ Flatshader (F)

Use: Filling, coloring, shading. Flat needles are groups of needles in which the individual needles lie parallel to each other. With flat needles, the last 8 - 14 mm up to the point are not soldered together. Most flat needles have 4 to 15 needles.

FLAT

▪ Needle grindings

The needle cut always refers to the individual needles of the needle groupings. The choice of needle cut depends on the respective area of application. For example, a shorter point allows more ink to be applied to the skin (good for filling work), but the skin is more irritated. With a longer tip, you get less ink into the skin, but the skin is less damaged (good for e.g. outlines/line work). The length of the cut also determines the shape of the resulting hole in the skin. This means that a long cut produces a narrow hole and a short cut produces a large hole. I use long taper for drawing lines and medium taper for filling work. The difference between the taper types is how steeply the needle is sharpened and where the sharpening starts. Some manufacturers also offer the Extra Long Taper or Super Long Taper, which is even steeper or sharper than the Long Taper. Round liner needles are only available from many manufacturers as long taper or super long taper. Flat needles are available in all bevel types. Soft Edge Magnum and Round Shader are usually only offered as Long Taper.

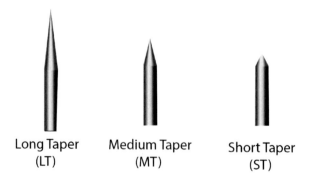

| Long Taper | Medium Taper | Short Taper |
| (LT) | (MT) | (ST) |

▪ Needle sizes

The individual needles in the needle groupings are available in different sizes. The higher the needle size, the more stress is placed on the skin during stitching. However, thicker needles also allow more color to be worked into the skin more quickly. I personally use two different sizes - 0.30 mm for drawing lines and 0.35 mm for filling and shading. Needle groupings can therefore not only have different needle grinds and arrangements, but also different needle sizes. Depending on the country, the needle sizes are indicated with different size specifications.

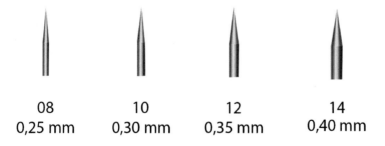

| 08 | 10 | 12 | 14 |
| 0,25 mm | 0,30 mm | 0,35 mm | 0,40 mm |

Accessories

- **ip selection for bobbin winding machines**

When using bar needles, you always need the right tip for the size and shape of the needle. First of all, a distinction is made between disposable and reusable tips. Disposable tips are, as the name suggests, only used once. They are usually made of plastic. If you choose disposable tips, you can also buy needles that already come with the appropriate disposable tip or grip. This saves you the hassle of searching for the right tip during preparation. Reusable tips are made of metal, but must be cleaned and sterilized after each use.

(DISPOSABLE TIP)   (REUSABLE TIP)   (TIPPED NEEDLE IN TIP)

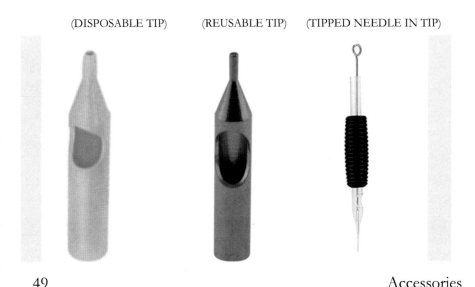

- **Consumables/equipment**

Please use disposable hygiene products only once and dispose of them properly, otherwise there is a risk of transmitting infectious diseases. Regularly check the expiration date of the disinfectants you use, as they lose their effectiveness over time.

- **Disposable cover material**

For the most common tools, machines and furniture, you can buy disposable plastic covers tailored to the respective size, e.g. for tattoo machines, wiping water bottles, couch covers, etc.

DISPOSABLE COVERING MATERIAL

- **Wooden mouth spatulas**

These spatulas are used to remove Vaseline or tattoo butter from the container. For hygienic reasons, a new wooden spatula must be used after each removal so that the containers are not contaminated with germs or similar.

- **Color caps**

Paint caps are available in different sizes, colors and shapes. I personally prefer transparent paint caps with anti-tip protection, which have a widened rim on the underside. To ensure a better grip of the paint cap, I always apply a little Vaseline to the underside of my paint caps and stick them to my disposable carpet pad on the work table. I always have different ink cap sizes in stock and choose the size of the caps depending on the size of the tattoo motif in order to have to dispose of as little ink residue as possible after tattooing. Always make sure that you fill the ink caps to the brim if possible, otherwise there is a risk of hitting the bottom of the ink cap with the needle when picking up the ink and damaging the needle. A damaged needle can injure the customer's skin.

WOODEN SPATULAS   (COLOR CAP W/O TILT PROTECTION)   (COLOR CAP WITH TILT PROTECTION)

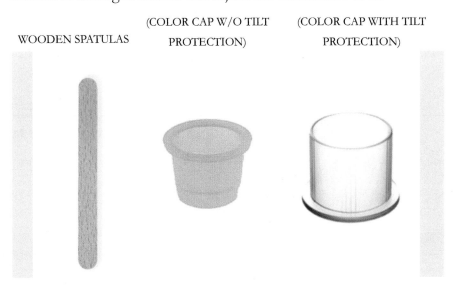

- **Tattoo inks**

Tattoo inks are applied under the skin using needles.

- **Ultrasonic cleaner**

Cleans paint residue, wound water, etc. from reusable accessories, even in hard-to-reach areas.

TATTOO INKS ULTRASONIC CLEANER

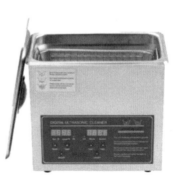

Accessories

- **Sterilizer**

Reusable accessories are sterilized by heat.

- **Disposable plastic cup**

The disposable cup, which has to be replaced for each customer, is filled with distilled water and is used to rinse the needles during tattooing.

STERILIZER   DISPOSABLE PLASTIC CUP

- **Stencil paper for hand drawing**

Stencil paper, also known as matrix paper, is used as a stencil to temporarily transfer a tattoo motif to the skin.

- **Stencil paper for thermo copiers**

Stencil paper for thermo copiers consists of several layers. It is inserted into the thermo copier with your template and creates exact copies and reproductions of your design. Although the thermal paper is designed for the thermal copier, it can also be used for hand drawing.

FOR HAND DRAWING   FOR THERMOCOPIER

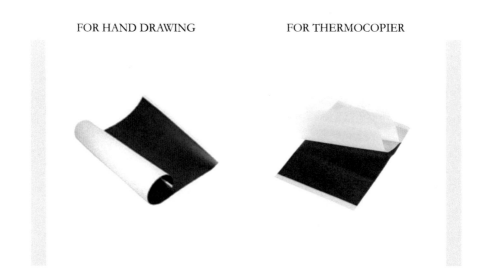

Accessories

- **Thermal copier**

A thermal copier is a very important tool in a tattoo studio, with the help of which the tattoo artist can quickly and easily convert an exact copy of his design into a transfer template. This technique saves a lot of time, as the design can be transferred to the customer's skin much faster with the help of a template than by drawing it freehand. Even if the customer is not satisfied with the positioning, the stencil can be reapplied at any time after the body area has been cleaned of the old design.

- **Synthetic skin / training skin**

Training skin is made from synthetic, skin-like material. It makes it possible to learn and improve skills without having to practise on real skin. Alternatively, you can also practice on bananas, oranges, pig skin or similar.

THERMAL COPIER   SYNTHETIC SKIN

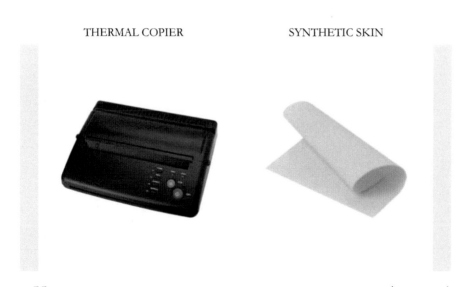

- **Grip tape**

The grip tape is wrapped around the handle of the tattoo machine to improve grip and thus ensure a better hold. Vibrations are dampened and the handle is not so heavily soiled.

- **Adhesive plaster**

Adhesive plaster can be used to attach the cling film around the finished tattoo motif or to fix the disposable work surface to the table to prevent it from slipping.

GRIP TAPE   ADHESIVE PLASTER

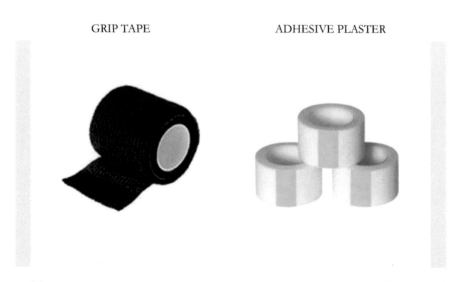

- **Needle disposal container**

These containers are used to safely dispose of used needles. They help to reduce the risk of infection and needlestick injuries.

- **Arm support**

An arm support can be used, among other things, to support the customer's arm during the tattooing process.

NEEDLE DISPOSAL CONTAINER   ARM SUPPORT

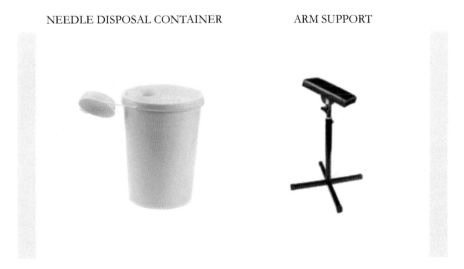

- **Paint stirrer**

The stirrer is used to mix paints.

- **Gloves**

Disposable gloves are essential for hygienic work. They are available in different colors, sizes and materials, such as latex, nitrile, vinyl, powdered and non-powdered.

STIRRER   GLOVES

- **Disposable razor**

So that the stencil adheres better to the skin and the tattoo does not become inflamed due to the hair, we need clean-shaven skin. As shaving irritates the skin, I shave my clients myself on the day of the tattoo.

- **Vaseline / tattoo butter**

The tattooing hand and needle glide better over the customer's skin when Vaseline or tattoo butter is applied and the applied stencil lasts longer on the skin. In addition, the customer's skin is easier to clean as a protective film forms over the skin and the ink is not absorbed into the skin. Compared to Vaseline, tattoo butter has the property that it supports wound healing during tattooing and reduces redness.

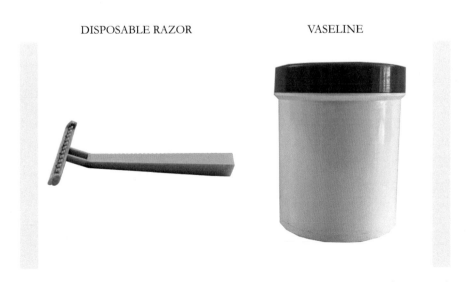

DISPOSABLE RAZOR
VASELINE

Accessories

- **Wound and healing ointment**

Wound and healing ointment supports the healing process and helps the skin to regenerate. I recommend an ointment with the active ingredient dexpanthenol.

- **Stripping fluid**

Stripping fluid serves as a solvent and is used to transfer the motif from the stencil paper to the skin.

WOUND AND HEALING OINTMENT   STRIPPING FLUID

- **Skin pens / skin doodlers**

The skin pen can be used to touch up or add to the stencil applied to the skin, to apply guide lines for optimum alignment of the tattoo motif and for freehand drawings on the skin.

- **Wiping cloths**

Wipes are used to wipe off excess ink from the skin during tattooing. When wiping, always make sure to wipe away from the stencil, otherwise there is a risk of damaging the stencil by wiping.

SKIN PENS/ SKIN DOODLERS   WIPING CLOTHS

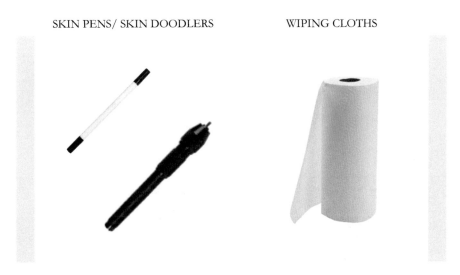

- **Nipple eyelets**

Nipple eyelets are disposable products and are used to reduce vibrations and secure the needle bar firmly in place.

- **Rubber band**

Rubber bands are disposable products and ensure that the needle bar runs smoothly.

NIPPLE EYELETS RUBBER BAND

Accessories

- **O-Ring**

O-rings cushion the hard blows of the armature bar on the contact screw.

- **Tattoo lamp**

A lamp is required for a good view during tattooing. If you are right-handed, the lamp should be on the left-hand side, and if you are left-handed, on the right-hand side so that no shadows are cast on the design. Some tattoo artists also work with headlamps.

O-RING   TATTOO LAMP

- **Distilled water**

Distilled water can be mixed with pH-neutral soap to clean the skin during tattooing. You can also pour distilled water into a disposable plastic cup, e.g. to rinse the needles during tattooing when switching between different colors. The water can also be used to dilute colors, e.g. for greywash. Before taking a break, I recommend rinsing the needle briefly so that the ink residue does not dry on the needle and it is more difficult for the needle to pick up ink when you resume work. Always use distilled water, as this is germ-free.

- **Skin disinfectant**

Skin disinfectant is required to disinfect your own hands before and after tattooing as well as the affected areas of the customer's skin before tattooing.

DISTILLED WATER   SKIND DISINFECTANT

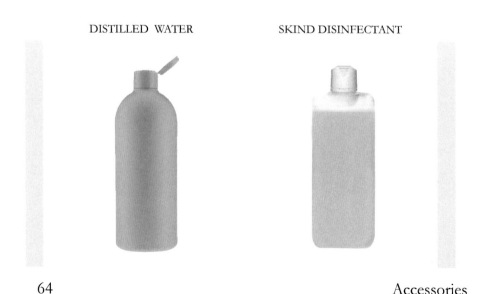

Accessories

- **pH-neutral soap / green soap**

During the session, the skin is cleaned with pH-neutral soap, e.g. to remove ink residue or wound water. Do not clean the tattoo with conventional soaps or shower gels. It is important to choose a soap that has a pH value of 5.5 (pH skin neutral) and does not contain perfume or alcohol.

- **Surface disinfectant**

A disinfectant is also required to disinfect all surfaces - in compliance with the specified contact time. All surfaces that you and the customer come into contact with during tattooing are disinfected. This also includes bottles and all equipment such as the customer couch, chair, work stool, work table, lamp and floors.

GREEN SOAP   SURFACE DISINFECTANT

- **Wound disinfectant**

Wound disinfectant is required to disinfect the freshly engraved tattoo motif.

- **Cling film**

The cling film is used to wrap everything that comes into direct contact with blood and wound water during tattooing to prevent cross-contamination (e.g. customer couch, chair, work stool, work table, lamp). After completion of the tattoo, all covered surfaces must still be disinfected again with surface disinfectant, as liquids may penetrate the cling film despite covering. The cling film also serves as a plaster for the finished tattoo motif. This prevents dirt or your own clothing from coming into contact with the freshly engraved tattoo and causing it to become infected.

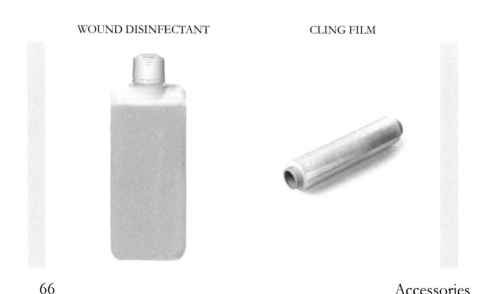

WOUND DISINFECTANT   CLING FILM

Accessories

▪ Stencil template remover

A stencil template remover can be used to remove a tattoo template from the skin if it is to be repositioned. It can also be used to remove remnants of the template.

STENCIL TEMPLATE REMOVER

Accessories

Power supply units / foot switches

Power supply units convert alternating current into direct current and supply the tattoo machines with power. Power supply units are used for both coil machines and rotary machines. The set voltage can be read on the display and adjusted as required by pressing the buttons. Power supply units are available in analog and digital versions. Depending on the model, different settings can be made, e.g. storage of operating voltage, stopwatch function for monitoring the session time, continuous operation (an operating mode in which there is no need to stop and start between pigmenting, the machine runs continuously), etc.

- **Analog power supply unit**

Analog power supply units have an analog voltage display, which can usually be adjusted using a rotary knob. Due to the analog design, the operating voltage can be read and adjusted less accurately than with digital devices.

STENCIL TEMPLATE REMOVER

1. Power cable
2. Analog volt display
3. Rotary knob for regulating the operating voltage
4. Foot switch connection
5. Tattoo machine connection
6. on/off button

- **Digital power supply unit**

Digital power supply units have a digital display on which various settings can be read and adjusted depending on the device. The digital display allows the operating voltage to be read and regulated more precisely.

1.   Digital volt display
2.   Stopwatch Power button
3.   Buttons for regulating the operating voltage
4.   Machine memory buttons (liner and shader)
5.   Power cable connection
6.   Tattoo machine connection
7.   Foot switch connection

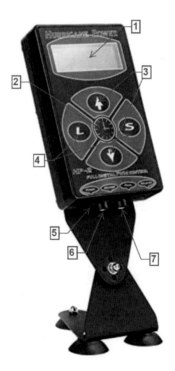

▪ Foot switch

Many power supply units require a foot switch to start the tattoo machine. However, some power supply units also have a button that takes over the function of the footswitch, making a footswitch unnecessary. Foot switches are available in different shapes and colors. I personally prefer the round shape, as the pressure point of the foot switch is in the middle and the appliance can therefore be operated from all sides.

SQUARE   ROUND

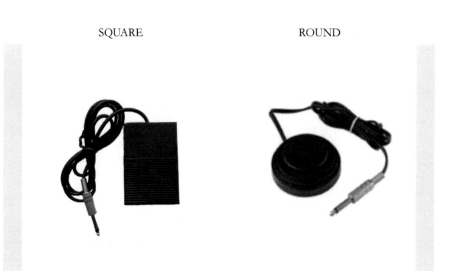

Coil machines

Tattoo machines are roughly divided into two categories due to their different functions and designs: Coil machines and rotary machines. There is no doubt that both rotary and coil machines can create fantastic tattoos. Both types of machines can produce the same result. Coil machines use electromagnetic current to create and break a circuit. This happens in a cyclical motion where the magnetic coils are electrically charged, causing the needle bar with the connected tattoo needle to pierce the skin. The downward movement of the needle bar interrupts the connection between the front spring and the contact screw and jumps back to the contact screw by means of the rear spring. The needle is pulled back into the end tube and the cycle starts again. Most coil machines are equipped with two solenoid coils. However, there are also machines with single solenoid coils or even three coils. The more coils there are, the more power can be generated. Among the coil machines, there are also machines that can be used universally (all-rounders), but in most cases, appropriate machines are set up and used individually for the different operations. These include, for example, liners (for drawing lines), shaders (for shading) and color packers (for filling color). Traditionally, bar needles are used for coil machines. Most tattoo artists who work with coil machines use several machines when tattooing, as changing the needle bars and tips is more time-consuming compared to conventional machines with needle modules. There are now adapter handles for coil machines so that they can be used with needle modules.

- **Advantages of coil machines**
- Low acquisition costs
- Adjustment of the stroke possible
- Various settings & repairs can be carried out by yourself

- **Disadvantages of coil machines**
  - High noise level
  - Strong vibrations
  - Many wearing parts
  - Heavy weight (not easy on the wrist)

- **Components of the coil machine**

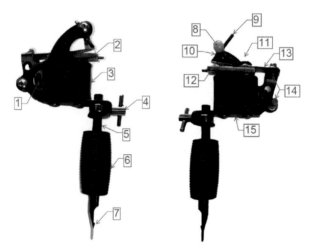

1. **Capacitor**
The main task of the capacitor is to reduce sparking at the contact point and to ensure that the coil machine runs smoothly.

2. **Contact block / Amature bar**
The contact block is used to hold the needle bars and sets the needle bar in motion.

3. **Solenoid coils / Coils**
The solenoid coils generate electromagnetic current.

4. **Adjusting screw / Tube Vice**
The adjusting screw fixes the handle to the tattoo machine.

Coil machines

5. Tailpipe / rear pipe / tube
The tailpipe is a tube attached to the grip and bolted to the frame.

6. Handle / Grip
The machine is held by the grip.

7. Tip
The needle protrudes from the tip.

8. Contact Screw Lock
This is used to adjust the angle of the contact screw.

9. Contact Screw
The contact screw is used to adjust the stroke.

10. Front binding
The contact screw is screwed into the contact thread to fix the set position.

11. O-Ring
The O-ring cushions the hard impacts of the armature bar on the contact screw.

12. Front Spring
Bending the front spring influences the speed, as the distance to the armature bar changes - this allows the working speed to be regulated.

13. Back Spring
The impact is determined by the rear spring: the more the spring is bent, the harder the machine runs.

14. Clip Cord connection / Rear Binding Post
The clip cord is connected to the clip cord connection.

15. Frame
The frame is the main element that holds everything together.

Mounting the bobbin machine

▪ Fitting the needle bar rubber
Take the machine and insert the needle bar rubber into the armature bar holder.

▪ Fit the O-ring
You can insert an O-ring to cushion the hard impacts of the armature bar on the contact screw. If the machine then runs too smoothly, this can be removed again.

FITTING THE NEEDLE BAR RUBBER   FIT O-RING

Coil machines

- **Fitting the tailpipe**

Take the grip piece, guide the tailpipe through the opening provided in the grip piece and tighten the existing screws to secure the tailpipe.

- **Fitting the tip**

Then insert the tip through the other opening of the handle and tighten the screws.

FITTING THE TAILPIPE   TFITTING THE TIP

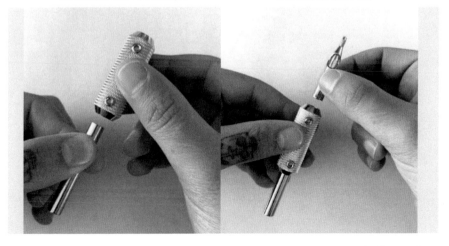

                                         Coil machines

- **Bending the needle bar**

To ensure that the needle bar is not unstable and straight lines can be drawn, the needle bar must be bent slightly so that the soldered needle tips can later rest in the tip.

- **Inserting the needle bar**

Take the bent needle bar and insert the tip through the end tube. Make sure that the soldered needle tips are pointing downwards.

BENDING THE NEEDLE BAR   INSERTING THE NEEDLE BAR

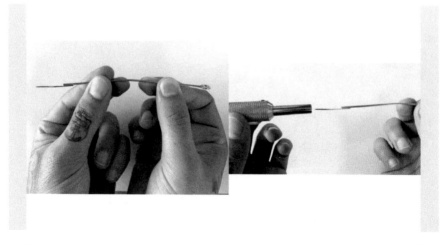

Coil machines

- **Fixing the handle**

Now insert the already fitted handle with the end pipe first through the opening on the frame of your bobbin winding machine and tighten the adjusting screw. Make sure that the open side of the tip is aligned towards the adjusting screw.

- **Fixing the needle bar to the armature bar**

Now fix the needle bar to the armature bar of your machine.

- **Attaching the machine rubber**

Then wrap the machine rubber around the frame of your machine and around the needle bar on the other side.

(DISPOSABLE TIP)   (REUSABLE TIP)   (TIPPED NEEDLE IN TIP)

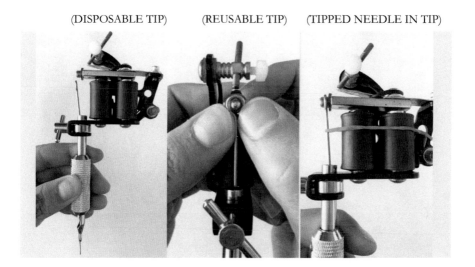

Coil machines

- **Visually check tip alignment**

Make sure that the open side of the tip is facing forwards.

- **Connecting the Clip Cord cable**

Now connect the clip cord cable to the clip cord connection on your machine.

VISUAL CONTROL   CONNECT CLIP CORD CABLE

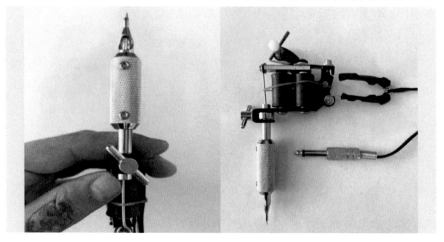

▪ Connecting the power supply unit

At the other end of the clip cord cable is the so-called jack plug. Connect this to your power supply unit. Then take the jack plug of your foot control and connect it to your power supply unit as well. Finally, connect one end of your mains cable to your power supply unit and the other end to the socket to supply the power supply unit with power.

CONNECT POWER SUPPLY UNIT

Coil machines

▪ Setting the needle protrusion

The needle protrusion is always adjusted while the needle is running. Activate your foot switch and loosen the adjusting screw on your tattoo machine until the handle comes loose.

Now push the handle upwards to increase the needle protrusion or downwards to reduce it. As soon as you have set the desired needle protrusion, fix it by tightening the adjusting screw. You can find out the exact needle protrusion in the chapter "Drawing, filling and shading lines".

ADJUST NEEDLE PROTRUSION

Coil machines

- **Alternative: Needle module adapter for bobbin machines**

As an alternative to bar needles, there are adapter grips for the use of needle modules. These also consist of an end tube and a grip piece. A rod is used for this, which is shaped like a bar needle and is guided through the opening of the end tube. Take the needle module and screw it into the handle piece. Attaching it to the bobbin winding machine and removing the needle are carried out in exactly the same way as with conventional needles.

- **Basic bobbin machine settings**

Each machine setting is individual and can vary from machine to machine. In the following steps, I will explain rough setting options. The sound of the machine should always be continuous and operation should run smoothly. You should therefore take sufficient time for the adjustment, as this will determine the quality of your work.

NEEDLE MODULE ADAPTER

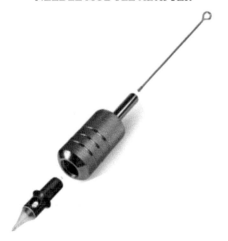

Coil machines

- **Adjusting the contact screw**

The position of the contact screw must be at 1 o'clock in order to have the optimum angle. This can be adjusted using the contact screw fastening. It is important that the contact screw rests on the front spring and makes contact with it. If the machine does not start or only starts poorly, screw the contact screw in further until the machine runs smoothly. As the contact screw at the contact point wears out over time, it must be readjusted from time to time so that it maintains contact with the front spring.

Coil machines

- **Stroke**

The stroke does not refer to the distance the needle protrudes from the tip, but to the distance the needle travels when moving up and down. The stroke can be adjusted by turning the contact screw, as the distance from the armature bar to the solenoid coil changes. The greater the distance (stroke), the stronger the needle beats during its upward and downward movement, as more distance is covered. The smaller the distance (stroke), the softer the machine beats. The following stroke settings are a rough guide:

- Shades 2.5 - 3.0 mm
- All-rounder 3.5 mm
- Lines and filling work 4 mm

- **Operating voltage**

Depending on the machine type and frequency, the average operating voltage of the power supply units is approximately

- Outlines: 9 volts
- Fill: 8 volts
- Shading: 7 Volt

Coil machines

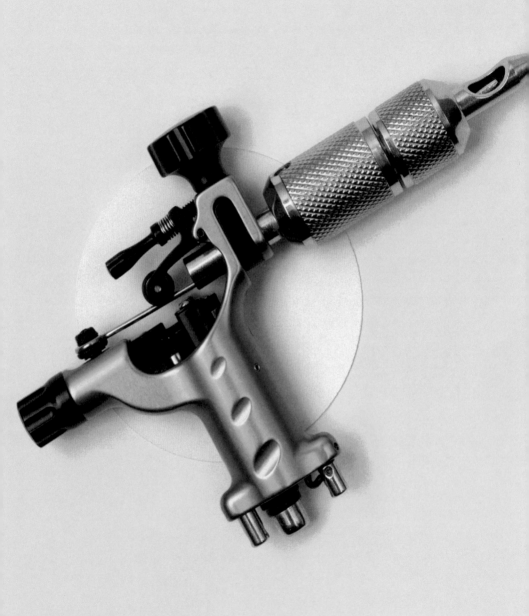

Rotary machines

A rotary tattoo machine usually has a small enclosed motor with a lifting disk/ball bearing that is directly connected to either a lifting rod or a tattoo needle. The motor moves the lifting disk in a circular motion, which in turn causes the needle bar to move up and down, thereby inserting the tips of the needle module or needle bars directly into the skin. As with the coil machine, there are also different variations and designs of rotary machines. Most are designed for use with needle modules, but there are also rotary machines that can be used with needle bars.

- **Advantages of the Rotary machine**
- Low volume
- Low vibration
- Needle protrusion adjustable by simply turning the handle
- Low weight and therefore easier on the wrist
- Less wear and tear
- Less cumbersome and generally easier to use

- **Disadvantages of the rotary machine**
- High acquisition costs
- Few adjustment options

- **Components of the rotary machine (battery-operated)**

1. On/and off button
Used to switch the machine on and off.

2. Control knobs for operating voltage
Used to regulate the operating voltage.

3. Rechargeable battery
The device has a replaceable rechargeable battery.

4. Needle projection adjustment
The needle protrusion can be adjusted by turning the handle.

5. Handle /grip
The machine is held by the handle.

6. Disposable needle module
 The needle module applies the color to the skin.

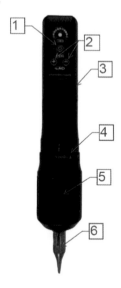

Rotary machines

- **Mounting the rotary machine**

- **Connect the battery**
Connect the battery to the machine.

- **Insert the needle module**
Insert the needle module and tighten it.

- **Setting the needle protrusion**
The needle protrusion is always set while the needle is running. On rotary machines, the needle protrusion can usually be adjusted by turning the handle.

CONNECT BATTERY   INSERT NEEDLE MODULE   NEEDLE ADJUSTMENT

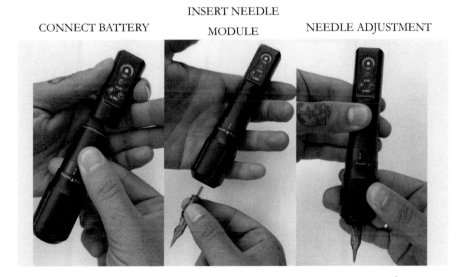

- **Rotary machine basic settings**

Nowadays, the majority of tattoo artists work with rotary machines. With most rotary machines, it is not possible to change individual device properties at will - as is the case with coil machines, for example. Therefore, hardly any settings need to be made. Each machine setting is individual and can therefore vary from machine to machine.

- **Stroke**

The stroke cannot be adjusted on most rotary machines, but the following also applies here: the greater the distance (stroke), the stronger the needle beats when moving up and down, as the needle covers more distance. The smaller the distance (stroke), the softer the machine beats. Before buying a tattoo machine, you should think carefully about which machine you would like to purchase. I recommend a tattoo machine with a stroke of 3.5 mm. These are considered all-rounder machines and are suitable for almost all tattoo styles. The following stroke numbers are a rough guide:

- Shades 2.5 - 3.0 mm
- All-rounder 3.5 mm
- Lines and filling work 4 mm

Operating voltage

Depending on the machine type and frequency, the average operating voltage of the power supply units is approx:

- Outlines: 11 Volt
- Filling: 9 Volt
- Shading: 7 Volt

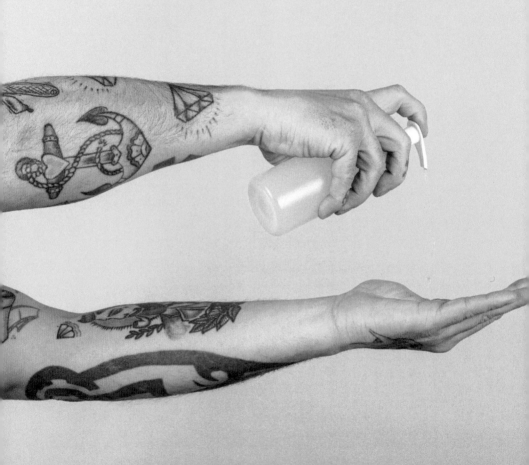

Hygiene

- **Hygienic working**

Hygiene measures help to protect against infectious diseases. When tattooing, there is constant contact with blood and wound water, which poses the risk of contracting infectious diseases such as HIV and hepatitis or transmitting them from customer to customer. Hygienic working practices are therefore essential. My recommendation is: consider and follow all hygiene measures as early as possible in the learning phase - even if you are only working on artificial skin or a similar surface at the beginning and cannot harm anyone. When you later work on people, it will be much easier for you to comply with the hygiene measures, as you will have already practised them during the learning phase on artificial skin and can now apply them routinely. The following procedures are part of hygienic working:

- **Customer preparation**
- Wash and disinfect hands and put on disposable gloves.
- Disinfecting the skin areas to be tattooed.
- Shaving the skin area with a disposable razor.

- **Preparation of the workstation**
- Cover the work table with foil or disposable underlays.
- Pack machines, cables, power supply unit, mop water bottle with disposable cover bags.
- Cover the customer couch with disposable sheets.
- Remove Vaseline/tattoo butter with disposable wooden spatula.
- Set up ink caps, shake inks and fill ink caps.
- Place the sterile disposable needles required for the motif on the work table and remove from the packaging in front of the customer and insert into the machine.

- **Working hygienically during tattooing**
- During the tattooing process, only the customer and the devices, machines, power supply units, wiping water, lamp, etc. required for tattooing are touched by the tattoo artist.
- As soon as anything else is touched, the gloves are contaminated and must be replaced with new, fresh disposable gloves. At the same time, however, the areas touched with the contaminated gloves are also contaminated and must be thoroughly cleaned and disinfected.
- From a hygiene point of view, remove your gloves to refill the paint and then put on fresh gloves.

- **Cleaning the workplace and equipment**
- Put on fresh disposable gloves.
- Dispose of all disposable plastic packaging, paint residues, paint caps, underlays, disposable sheets from the customer couch, etc.
- Dispose of needles in the needle disposal container.
- Disinfect the customer couch, work table, all surfaces, lamp, power supply unit, cable, tattoo machine and handle, taking into account the appropriate contact time. Contact times are marked on the bottles of the disinfectant to be used.
- Needle modules are generally equipped with a membrane that prevents ink and wound fluid from entering the handle, so it is usually sufficient to disinfect the handle with surface disinfectant. However, most rotary machine handles are autoclavable and can be cleaned in a sterilizer.
- When using reusable materials such as tips, tubes and grips, these must first be thoroughly cleaned in an ultrasonic bath to remove paint residues and stubborn dirt, even in inaccessible areas. They must then be sterilized in an autoclave.
- Disposable tubes, tips and grips are disposed of.

Tattoo aftercare

A tattoo is a wound and should be treated accordingly. To ensure that your customer can enjoy their new tattoo for a long time, I recommend that you provide your customer with care instructions. The better the tattoo is cared for during the healing phase, the more beautifully the tattoo will heal and the easier it will be to avoid any re-stitching or inflammation.

- **After the tattooing**

The foil bandage should be removed 2-3 hours after tattooing. It is not advisable to wear plastic bandages for too long, as the warm, moist environment can create a perfect breeding ground for germs and bacteria.

- **Washing and cleaning**

The tattoo must be washed thoroughly until it is free of wound secretions, ink and cream residue. The tattoo must be dabbed with a clean, tear-resistant paper towel and left to air dry for approx. 15 minutes. The tattoo must not be cleaned with conventional soaps or shower gels. A soap with a pH value of 5.5 (pH skin neutral) should be used that does not contain perfume or alcohol. The tattoo should be washed approx. two to three times a day during the first week, preferably in the morning, at midday and in the evening. If the tattoo is exposed to a lot of dust and dirt in everyday life (e.g. construction work etc.), it is advisable to clean the tattoo several times a day with clean hands and to protect it with long clothing. Bathing in lakes, the sea or swimming pools is not advisable, as this can lead to wound infections.

- **Creams**

The tattoo should be creamed regularly and in good doses during the healing phase. If the tattoo oozes at the beginning, the exuding wound secretion must always be washed off before applying cream. If too little cream is applied, a crust may form, which can lead to loss of color or even scarring. Applying cream too often or too thickly can lead to softening of the skin, which can result in loss of color and inflammation. There are various tattoo creams on the market for wound care.

- **Protection from contamination**

Sweat and dirt can lead to inflammation, which is why it is important to keep the wound as clean as possible and to avoid sports and other sweaty activities for the time being. Clothing that is too tight or fluffy should also be avoided. If the clothing sticks to the tattoo, it is advisable not to simply remove it, but to soak the affected area with water until the clothing detaches from the tattoo on its own.

- **Avoid the sun / solarium**

Newly tattooed skin burns much faster in the sun than healthy skin, which is why it is best not to expose the new tattoo to sunlight (including solariums) for four to six weeks.

- **Itchiness**

It is normal for a slight scab to form during the healing process. This must not be scraped off. Scarring and loss of color would be the result. The scab will peel off by itself after a certain time. The first layer of skin has formed underneath. This new layer of skin is still very thin and is often slightly shiny, which is why it is also called "silver skin". This phase can last a few weeks and can also cause itching. Here too, it is important not to scratch and to continue applying cream. The tattoo should be completely healed in around six weeks.

Allergies

- **Allergy to tattoo ink**

An allergy to tattoo ink is a contact allergy in which those affected are allergic to the ingredients contained in the tattoo ink. Tattoo products are mixtures of pigments and additives, e.g. solvents, surfactants, binding agents, preservatives, fragrances and plant extracts. Possible impurities - e.g. traces of nickel, cobalt and chromate - can also cause allergies. If the ink is injected under the skin, it usually takes a few hours or even days before the first symptoms appear. This results in inflammation of the skin, which is often accompanied by itching, redness, swelling, burning, spots or blisters. Those affected should consult a doctor as soon as possible if they experience symptoms. The following substances have a particularly high allergic potency:

- Red: manganese, mercury and cadmium
- Brown: iron oxide and cadmium
- Yellow: cadmium
- Green: chromium
- Blue: cobalt compounds

Complications can occur, especially with tattoos with color pigments, but black tattoos usually do not cause any problems.

- **Latex allergy**

Latex allergies are also a contact allergy that can be caused by the tattoo artist's gloves, for example. On contact with latex, the skin at the point of contact can become red, itchy and burn. If your client is allergic to latex, you can use vinyl or nitrile gloves as an alternative.

Tattooing, that you should avoid

As a serious and responsible tattoo artist, you should refrain from tattooing certain people. Young people, for example, should not be tattooed before they reach the age of majority due to health, social and aesthetic risks. Teenagers are still growing, which means that a tattoo will change in length and width as the body expands. Teenagers often do not give enough thought to the motif or the part of the body to be tattooed. This can make it more difficult for them to choose a career, as many companies require their employees to have a neutral appearance. People who are under the influence of drugs, alcohol or anticoagulant medication should also not be tattooed, as these substances have a blood-thinning effect. The affected skin area could bleed more and absorb the ink less well during tattooing, which can significantly impair the quality of the tattoo. Alcohol and drugs also have an anaesthetic effect and therefore impair general perception and decision-making. You should also not tattoo people who wish to have discriminatory, anti-constitutional symbols or similar tattooed. Respect for other people shows the quality of your personality.

▪ Tattooing during pregnancy
You should not tattoo pregnant or breastfeeding women for the following reasons:

▪ Changed perception of pain
When a woman is pregnant, her body is in an exceptional state. The hormonal change affects almost all areas, including the skin and connective tissue. Experts agree that pregnant women have an altered perception of pain, which can make a tattoo much more uncomfortable.

- **Danger of premature labor**

In the worst case scenario, the pain could trigger premature labor and thus a premature birth. In general, particularly stressful situations during pregnancy can lead to premature birth.

- **Carcinogenic substances in tattoo inks**

Some tattoo inks contain polycyclic aromatic hydrocarbons. These are considered carcinogenic and an unborn baby should not be exposed to them.

- **Wound healing problems**

A tattoo is an open wound on the body through which bacteria can penetrate. There is always the possibility of wound healing problems, as fresh tattoos can easily become infected. These are complications that should be avoided, especially during pregnancy. A doctor would have to prescribe antibiotics in the event of inflammation and not all preparations are permitted during pregnancy.

- **Changed body proportions**

Due to water retention and loose connective tissue as well as additional weight, the skin is stretched differently in many areas during pregnancy and is subject to greater stress than normal. The proportions change, sometimes permanently. Even after the birth, it can take several months to return to normal. If the "base" of the skin warps, lettering can become crooked, for example, and images can appear puffy or unintentionally thin - depending on how the area where the tattoo was applied during pregnancy changes.

▪ Getting tattoos while breastfeeding

Tattoos should also be avoided while breastfeeding. This is because small amounts of tattoo ink are also transferred to breast milk. Whether and what effects the substances contained, such as nickel or polycyclic aromatic hydrocarbons (carcinogenic), can have on the child has not yet been investigated. However, allergic reactions to the baby, for example, are conceivable.

Tattooing, that you should avoid

Stencil

Always take enough time to create and apply the stencil. A poorly or incorrectly applied stencil can blur, disappear completely or warp during the tattooing process. Always make sure that your customer stands upright and adopts as natural a posture as possible when applying the stencil. If you apply the stencil in an unnatural posture - such as on a lying or sitting customer - the motif will distort in the natural posture due to different body proportions. An incorrectly applied stencil can be removed using a stencil template remover.

- **Attaching the stencil**
- When using stencil paper for hand drawing, place the stencil paper on a surface with the color layer facing upwards.

ATTACHING THE STENCIL

- Now place the paper with the motif on the matrix paper. Staple the sheets together to prevent the paper with your motif from slipping. Now trace the contours of your motif with a pen, applying light pressure. This will create a copy of your motif on the back of your template.
- This is your finished template. Now release the clips and lift off your template.

ATTACH MOTIF   FINISHED TEMPLATE

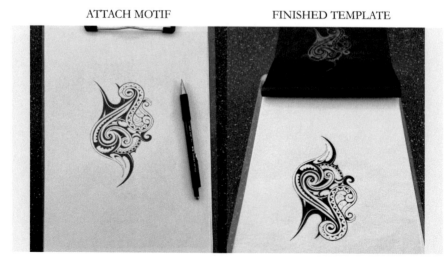

Stencil

- Now you can cut away the excess paper approx. 5 cm around the contours of the motif. If you are attaching the motif to an uneven area of skin, such as the arm, cut all the way around the template. This will release the tension in the paper and the template can be placed more precisely around the arm.

CUT AWAY EXCESS   CUT IN TEMPLATE

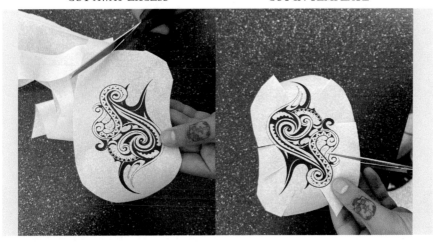

Stencil

- Now shave the area of skin onto which the motif is to be transferred and moisten it with a suitable solvent, e.g. drawing fluid, and press the template firmly onto the skin with the color layer. When transferring motifs with stencil paper, you need to use a little sensitivity with regard to the solvent. Only apply enough so that the skin is only slightly moistened. If the template runs on your skin after application, this is an indication of too much solvent. If the print is barely visible on the skin, you may have applied too little solvent.

- Now remove the paper and allow the solvent to evaporate.

- When practicing on artificial skin, you should always use stencil paper for hand drawing.

APPLY MOTIF   PEEL OFF PAPER

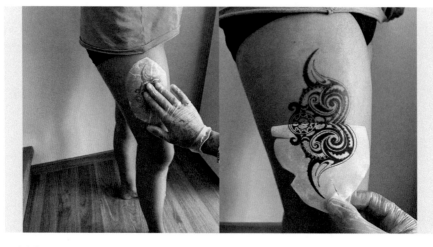

- **Bloodlines**

Bloodlines do not use contour lines. This is the case when a motif is to appear more realistic and lively and consists mainly of shading (e.g. portraits). With the exception that only very diluted color is used for the contours when engraving, the other work processes for contour lines remain the same. Bloodlines are used to secure the stencil. The outlines then consist of the redness of the skin/blood or of barely visible lines using highly diluted color. Bloodlines are usually engraved with a fine round liner needle (1 or 3).

BLOODLINES

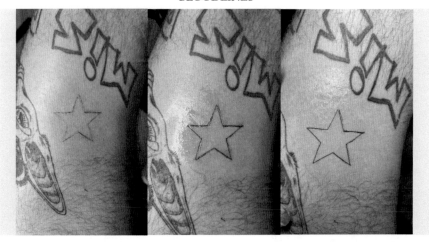

Stencil

Body posture

The tattoo artist's body is always positioned so that they have a good view of the needle. Right-handers therefore usually sit leaning slightly forward to the left with their head turned to the right so as not to block their view of the stencil and needle with their own hand. The opposite is usually true for left-handers.

- **Body positions of the customer**

Always try to position the customer so that the area of skin to be tattooed is as flat as possible. This way you do not have to work against gravity. If possible, the customer should stretch the area to be tattooed with their posture. This can be achieved by positioning the customer differently or by tilting the body to create tension on the surface of the skin. It is important that the client sits or lies in such a way that you can work comfortably. Below I will show you the positions in which I usually tattoo the most common body parts.

FRONT SIDE: NECK   SIDE: NECK

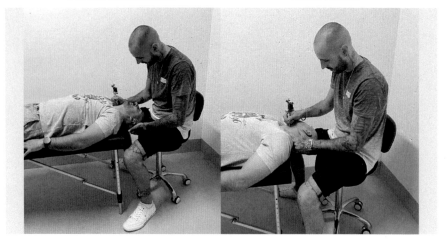

NECK   RIBS

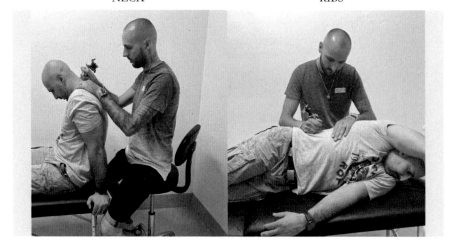

Body posture

OUTSIDE: FOREARM   INSIDE: FOREARM

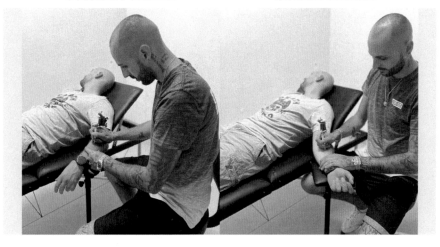

BELLY   HEAD

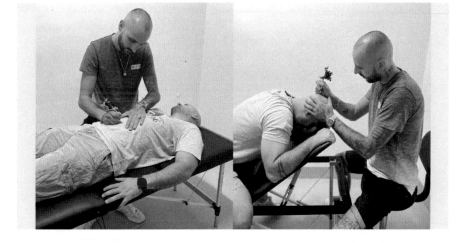

Body posture

FACE   WADE

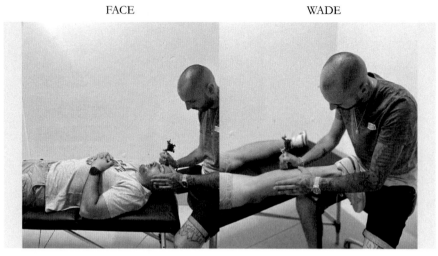

OUTSIDE: UPPER ARM   INSIDE: UPPER ARM

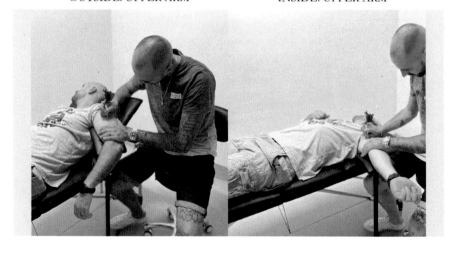

                                       Body posture

BACKSIDE: UPPER ARM   BACKSIDE: FOREARM

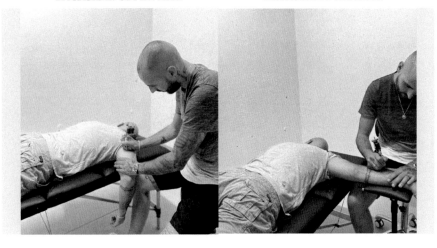

HAND   FOOT

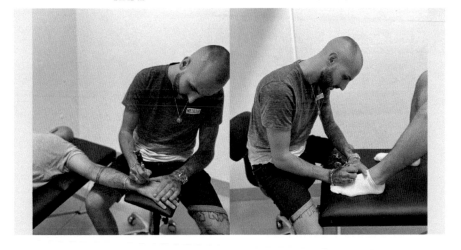

Body posture

▪ Tensioning the skin

Keeping the skin under tension when tattooing is extremely important. If the skin is not or not sufficiently taut, the skin cannot absorb enough ink when filling or shading, for example. Lines cannot be drawn cleanly or the skin does not absorb the ink properly. I stretch the skin with my index finger and thumb. Depending on the nature of the connective tissue, some parts of the body stretch almost automatically - such as the calf or forearm. Other parts of the body, on the other hand, are so slack - such as the inner upper arm or stomach - that the ball of the tattooing hand has to support the stretching. This is done by pulling the ball of the hand outwards during tattooing, creating a taut surface.

SKIN TENSION

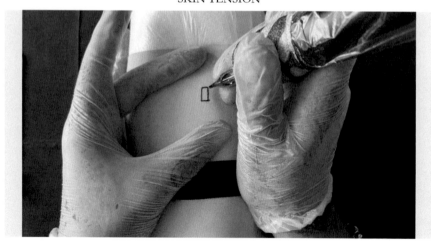

Body posture

Drawing lines

Drawing lines needs to be practiced. If your lines are shaky at first, don't worry. This will improve with time and practice. Clean lines are drawn from the wrist, with the ball of the hand resting firmly on the client to prevent possible trembling. For very long lines, the needle should be gently lifted out of the line before the hand starts to shake. Reposition the ball of your hand and pick up the line again. I always hold my breath just before placing the needle on the skin while drawing the line - this helps me to prevent trembling. As soon as I have drawn the line, I continue breathing. The needle is always pulled behind the hand and not pushed. Draw the lines slowly, but continuously, and try to draw the lines in one piece if possible and only put them down when necessary. If you are right-handed, always start the tattoo in the bottom right-hand corner and if you are left-handed, in the left-hand corner. This ensures that the stencil is not smudged by the ball of your hand when tattooing.

Before you start with the first line, spread some vaseline on the line you want to tattoo as well as on the underside of your middle finger. This will allow the tattoo to glide better over the skin. The other hand holds the wipe and stretches the skin. After each line you draw, wipe off the excess ink on the skin to get a good view of the stencil and thus of the lines to be drawn. Also make sure that you always brush away from the stencil when wiping off the paint so as not to smudge the stencil and make it unrecognizable. Vaseline must be applied after each new line and new paint must be applied to the needle tips. Try to draw each line from the perfect position for you. If necessary, change your posture or sitting position or reposition the client.

When drawing lines, there are basically the following options for working:

- **Machine angle**

When drawing lines, I work at an angle of approx. 90 degrees to the skin.

- **Protrusion of the needle when working with mounted tips**

When working in place, the needle is left protruding from the tip exactly as far as it should penetrate the skin. This is approx. 0.9-1.5 millimetres. The tip then rests on the skin when pricking. The advantage of this is that the stitch depth does not have to be adjusted by hand. The disadvantage is the poor or non-existent view of the needle, which is already blurred due to the wound fluid, vaseline and color residue.

MACHINE ANGLE   NEEDLE STAND

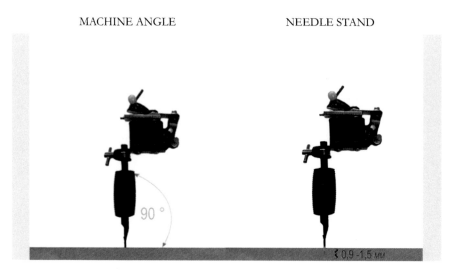

Drawing lines

▪ Needle protrusion when working on the fly

When working on the fly, the needle protrudes much further from the tip than it actually penetrates the skin. The tip is therefore not placed on the skin, but protrudes approx. 2 millimetres. When tattooing, the needle only penetrates 0.9-1.5 millimeters deep. This means that you will always see approx. 1.1-0.5 millimeters of the needle. The advantage of working in this way is that the needle remains visible and the stencil is not missed when piercing. This allows you to work much more precisely. On the other hand, working on the fly is technically more demanding, as the stitch depth must be regulated continuously. Hold the handle of the machine between your thumb and index finger, with the tip resting on your middle finger. The attached tip guides the entire machine on the skin, so always apply vaseline to the underside of your middle finger so that it can glide better over the skin. The tip on the middle finger makes it easy to regulate the stitch depth. You can use your middle finger to apply a little pressure to the customer's skin to maintain stability when guiding the needle.

NEEDLE PROTRUSION WHEN WORKING ON THE FLY

2,0 мм ⟨ ⟩ 1,1 мм
0,9 мм

Drawing lines

▪ Training plan for drawing lines

To help you prepare for the human skin step by step, I have drawn up a training plan for you. Here you will develop a feel for the tattoo machine, train your eye-hand coordination and learn how to stretch the skin, draw lines and pick them up. If you are unsure at any point, simply read the relevant chapter again. Practice continuously for an hour a day and you will make rapid progress.

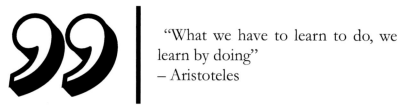

"What we have to learn to do, we learn by doing"
– Aristoteles

Drawing lines

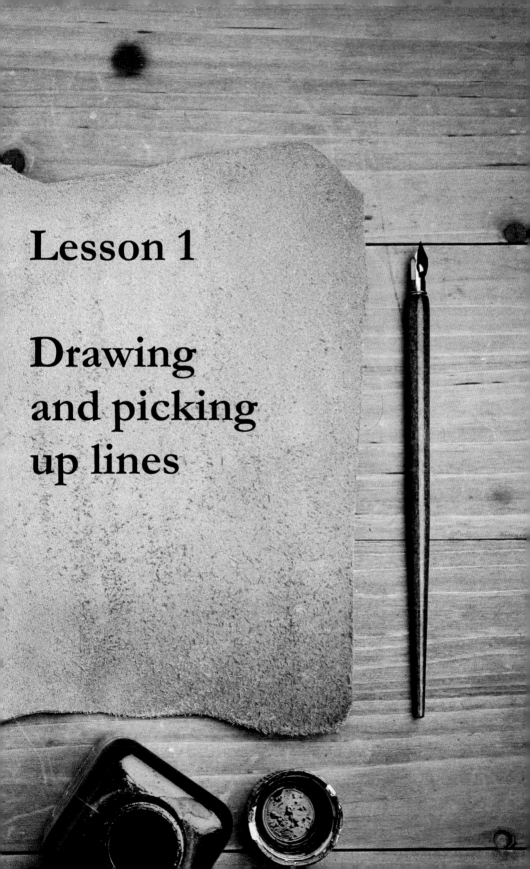

Lesson 1

Drawing
and picking
up lines

- **Step 1**

Take a piece of copy paper and place it crosswise in front of you. Then use a pencil and ruler to draw several lines of different lengths vertically and horizontally on the paper.

- **Step 2**

Use the fineliner to start tracing the lines you have drawn with the pencil. Make sure that the heel of your hand is always resting on the paper and try to draw the lines as long as possible without putting the pencil down. As soon as you notice that you are getting shaky, stop the line and reposition the ball of your hand. Now pick up the line again, but not directly at the point where you ended it, but a little before so that the transitions run smoothly into each other. The paper must remain on the table and must not be turned to suit your needs. Simulate stretching the skin on the paper with your hand. Always practice as realistically as possible, as if you were working on a customer. Repeat the exercise for an hour.

STEP 1   STEP 2

Draw lines

Lesson 2

Practicing parallels

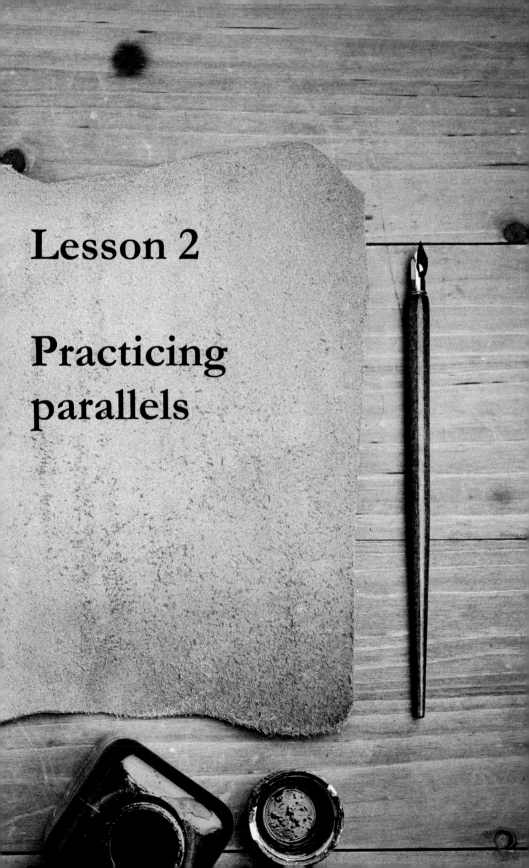

- **Step 1**

Take a piece of copy paper and place it crosswise in front of you. Then use a pencil and ruler to draw several parallel lines vertically and horizontally next to each other on the paper.

- **Step 2**

Use the fineliner to start tracing the lines you have drawn with the pencil. Make sure that the heel of your hand is always on the ground and try to draw the lines as long as possible without putting the pencil down. As soon as you notice that you are getting shaky, stop the line and reposition the ball of your hand. Now pick up the line again, but not directly at the point where you ended it, but just before, so that the transitions run smoothly into each other. The paper must remain on the table and must not be turned to suit your needs. Simulate stretching the skin on the paper with your hand. Always practice as realistically as possible, as if you were working on a customer. When tattooing parallel lines, make sure that as a right-handed person you draw the lines from left to right so that your hand does not block your view and the ball of your hand does not smudge the stencil. If no parallel lines are tattooed, right-handers always start from the bottom right of the motif to the left. Left-handers from the bottom left to the right. Repeat the practice for one hour.

STEP 1   STEP 2

132   Draw lines

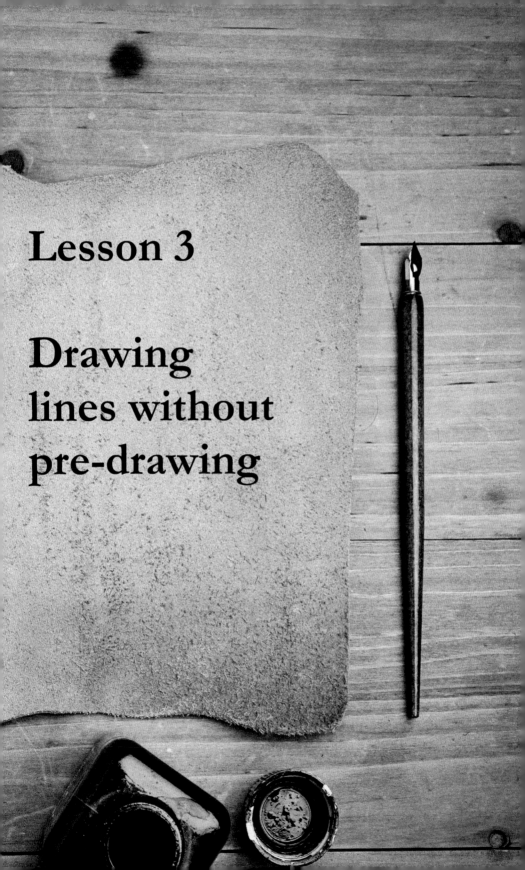

Lesson 3

Drawing
lines without
pre-drawing

▪ Step 1

Take a piece of copy paper and place it crosswise in front of you. Then draw several long lines vertically and horizontally on the paper freehand using a fineliner. Make sure that the heel of your hand is always on the paper and try to draw the lines as long as possible without putting the pen down. As soon as you notice that you are getting shaky, stop the line and move the ball of your hand. Now pick up the line again, but not directly at the point where you ended it, but just before, so that the transitions run smoothly into each other. The paper must remain on the table and must not be turned to suit your needs. Simulate stretching the skin on the paper with your hand. Always practice as realistically as possible, as if you were working on a customer. Repeat the practice for an hour.

STEP 1

Draw lines

Lesson 4

Practicing circles

• Step 1

Take a piece of copy paper and place it crosswise in front of you. Use a pair of compasses to draw several circles of different sizes on the paper.

• Step 2

Then start tracing the circles drawn with the compass using a fineliner. Make sure that the heel of your hand is always resting and try to draw the circles in one stretch for as long as possible without putting the pen down. As soon as you notice that you are getting shaky, end the line and reposition the ball of your hand. Now pick up the line again, but not directly at the point where you ended it, but just before, so that the transitions run smoothly into each other. The paper must remain on the table and must not be turned to suit your needs. Simulate stretching the skin on the paper with your hand. Always practice as realistically as possible, as if you were working on a customer. Repeat the practice for an hour.

STEP 1   STEP 2

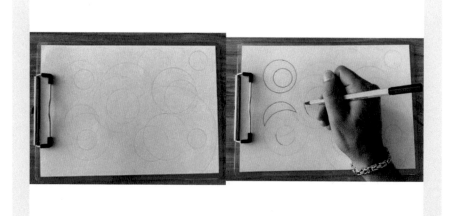

Draw lines

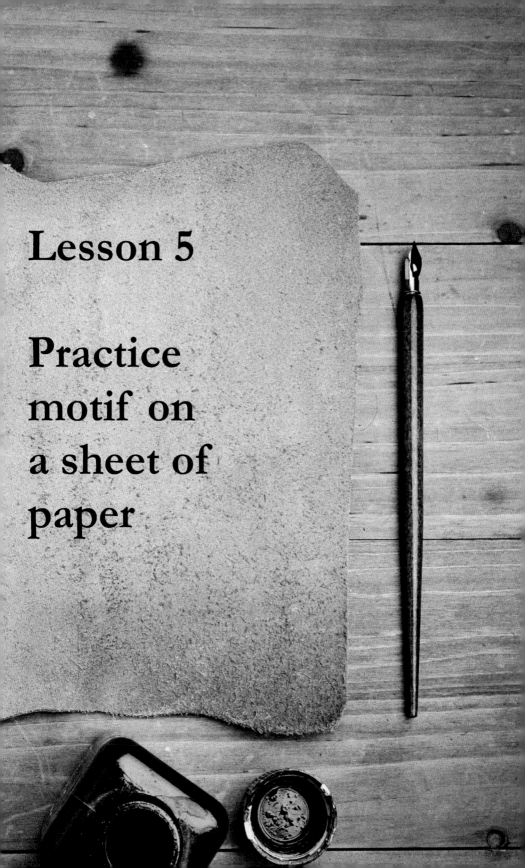

Lesson 5

Practice motif on a sheet of paper

- **Step 1**

Draw a motif on a sheet of paper with a pencil or print out a motif.

- **Step 2**

Use a fineliner to start tracing the motif you have drawn or printed in pencil. Make sure that the heel of your hand is always on the ground and try to draw the lines as long as possible without putting the pencil down. As soon as you notice that you are getting shaky, finish the line and move the ball of your hand. Now pick up the line again, but not directly at the point where you ended it, but just before, so that the transitions run smoothly into each other. The paper must remain on the table and must not be turned to suit your needs. Simulate stretching the skin on the paper with your hand. Always practice as realistically as possible, as if you were working on a customer. Repeat the practice for an hour.

STEP 1   STEP 2

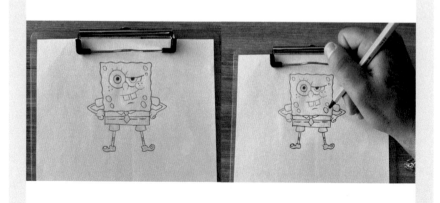

Draw lines

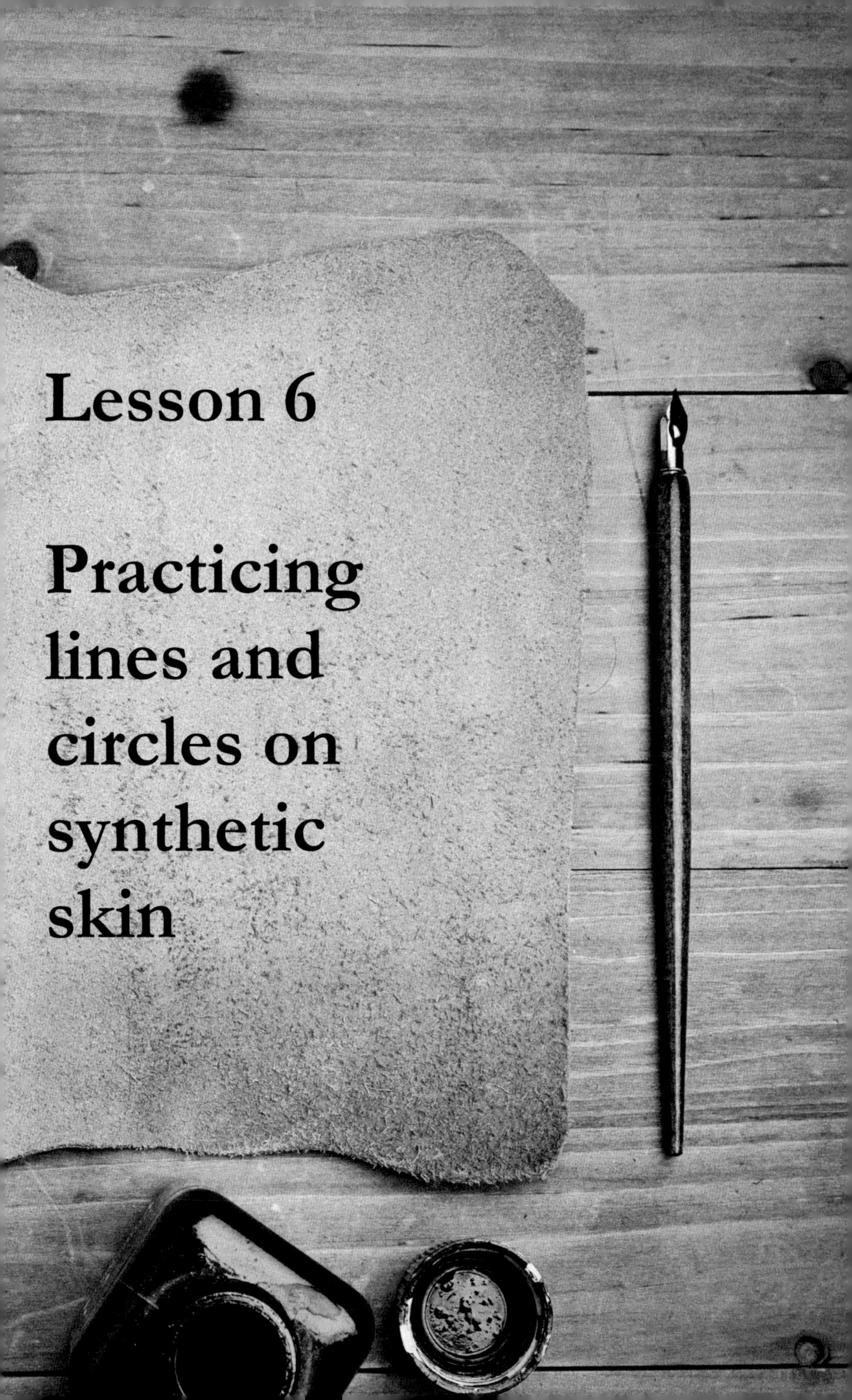

Lesson 6

Practicing
lines and
circles on
synthetic
skin

▪ Step 1

Take synthetic skin and place it in front of you. Synthetic skin must always be cleaned beforehand so that the stencil lifts. Use a ruler and a pen to draw several lines vertically and horizontally on the artificial skin. Use a circle stencil or similar to draw circles on the artificial skin.

▪ Step 2

Now apply vaseline to the lines to be tattooed. Use the tattoo machine to start tattooing the lines and circles drawn on the artificial skin. You can use a size 7 RL ø 0.35 needle for this task. Make sure that the heel of your hand is always resting on the skin and try to draw the lines as long as possible in one go without putting the machine down. As soon as you notice that you are getting shaky, stop the line and reposition the ball of your hand. Now pick up the line again, but not directly at the point where you ended it, but just before, so that the transitions run smoothly into each other. The artificial skin must remain on the table and must not be turned to suit your needs. Use your hand to simulate stretching the skin on the artificial skin. Always practice as realistically as possible, as if you were working on a client. Repeat the practice for one hour.

STEP 1 STEP 2

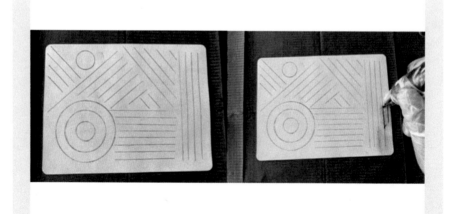

Draw lines

Lesson 7

Practice motif on curves with artificial skin

- **Step 1**

Take artificial skin and place it over a kitchen roll or similar. This simulates the curve of an arm or leg. Artificial skin must always be cleaned beforehand so that the stencil lifts. Create a motif on stencil paper and apply it to the artificial skin. Wait approx. 20 minutes until the stencil is dry and only then start tattooing. The stencil does not lift as well on artificial skin as it does on human skin.

- **Step 2**

Now apply vaseline to the lines to be tattooed. Use the tattoo machine to start tattooing the outlines of your stencil. You can use a size 7 RL ø 0.35 needle for this task. Make sure that the heel of your hand is always resting and try to draw the lines as long as possible in one go without putting the machine down. As soon as you notice that you are getting shaky, stop the line and reposition the ball of your hand. Now pick up the line again, but not directly at the point where you ended it, but just before, so that the transitions run smoothly into each other. The artificial skin must remain on the table above the kitchen roll and must not be turned to suit your needs. Simulate stretching the skin on the artificial skin with your hand. Always practice as realistically as possible, as if you were working on a customer. Repeat the practice for an hour.

STEP 1   STEP 2

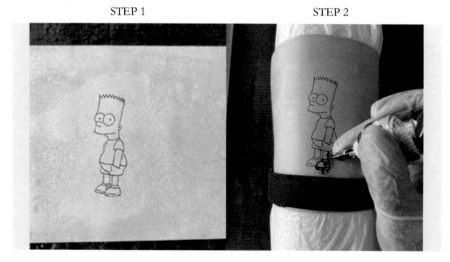

Draw lines

Filling

Blotchy, incompletely filled areas look unprofessional. The same procedure always applies to all needle configurations in order to ensure that the area is filled completely. Stitch in adjacent lanes and always overlap the already filled lane with circular movements, regardless of the needle type. Keep the circles narrow and small. For a better view, work from right to left if you are right-handed and from left to right if you are left-handed - or from top to bottom - to ensure a better view of the area to be filled. The palm of the tattooing hand should also always be on top. When filling in colors, it is important to follow a certain sequence. The colors are always tattooed from dark to light. This means that the black areas of a tattoo are always filled first. This is followed by the next lighter color. Towards the end, colors such as pink and yellow are added and white comes at the end. As the pores of the skin are opened by the needle pricks during tattooing, there is a risk that the excess color will be wiped into the finished tattooed areas of skin. The skin should also be cleaned of ink residue from other colors after each color change. The same technique applies when working in color tones as when working in different shades of black.

BLOTCHY TATTOO   CIRCULAR MOVEMENTS SIDE BY SIDE

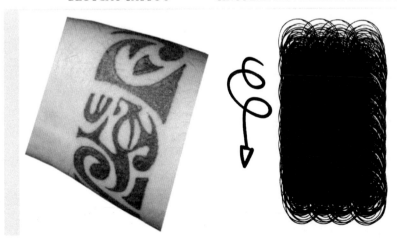

- **Machine angle**

When filling surfaces with magnum needles, I work at an angle of 40-50 degrees to the skin. When filling with round shaders, I work at an angle of approx. 90 degrees.

- **Needle protrusion when working with the tip fitted**

When filling, I almost always work with the tip in place. When working with the tip in place, you leave the needle sticking out of the tip exactly as far as it should penetrate the skin, i.e. approx. 0.9-1.5 millimetres. The tip then rests on the skin when piercing. In contrast to working on the fly, I do not use the middle finger as a guide. As I always place the tip completely on the skin when filling, i.e. I insert the needle completely into the skin, I do not need the middle finger as a guide. I am also much more agile without the middle finger. As circular movements are made when filling, the hand must be as flexible as possible. You hold the handle between your thumb and forefinger like a pen.

ANGLE MAGNUM NEEDLES   ANGLE ROUND SHADER NEEDLES

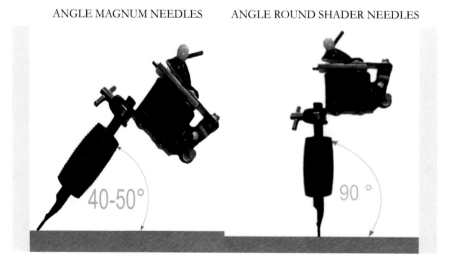

Filling

• Needle protrusion when working on the fly

I usually fill small areas with a round shader. In this case, I work on the fly because of the better visibility. When working on the fly, the needle is left sticking out of the tip much further than it is actually inserted into the skin. The tip is therefore not placed on the skin, but sticks out about 2 millimeters. When tattooing, it only penetrates 0.9-1.5 millimeters deep. This means that you will always see approx. 1.1-0.5 millimeters of needle.

NEEDLE WHEN WORKING WITH
THE NEEDLE IN PLACE

NEEDLE WHEN WORKING ON THE
FLY

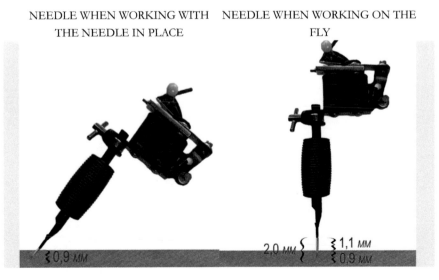

Filling

- **Training plan for filling areas**

This training plan will help you, among other things, to fill areas opaquely, train eye-hand coordination and stretch the skin. Carefully consider and implement all the skills you have learned in the previous chapters in the training plan. If you are unsure about something, read the relevant chapter again. Practice continuously for an hour a day and you will make rapid progress.

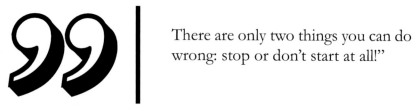

There are only two things you can do wrong: stop or don't start at all!"

Filling

Lesson 1

Filling a small area with a RS

- **Step 1**

Take artificial skin and place it over a kitchen roll or similar. This simulates the curve of an arm or leg. Artificial skin must always be cleaned beforehand so that the stencil lifts. Draw several small areas of approx. 1.0 x 0.5 cm on the artificial skin with a pen and apply Vaseline to the area to be tattooed. Prick the outlines with the tattoo machine.

- **Step 2**

Fill the area on the fly - for better visibility in small areas - with a 9 RS ø 0.35 needle. Make sure that the heel of your hand is always in contact with the surface. The artificial skin must remain on the table above the kitchen roll and must not be turned to suit your needs. Simulate stretching the skin on the artificial skin with your hand. Always practice as realistically as possible, as if you were working on the customer. Repeat the practice for an hour.

STEP 1 · · · · · · · · · · · · · · · · · · · STEP 2

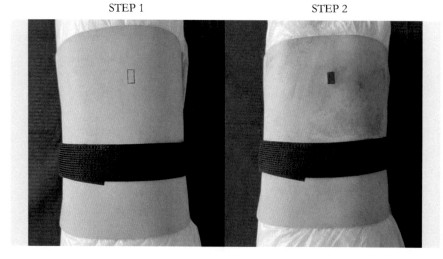

Filling

Lesson 2

Filling a small area with a RL

- **Step 1**

Take artificial skin and place it over a kitchen roll or similar. This simulates the curve of an arm or leg. Artificial skin must always be cleaned beforehand so that the stencil lifts. Draw several small areas of approx. 1.0 x 0.5 cm on the artificial skin with a pen. Now apply vaseline to the area to be tattooed and engrave the outlines.

- **Step 2**

Fill the area on the fly with a 9 mm RL ø 0.35 needle for better visibility in small areas. Make sure that the heel of your hand is always in contact with the surface. The artificial skin must remain on the table above the kitchen roll and must not be turned to suit your needs. Simulate stretching the skin on the artificial skin with your hand. Always practice as realistically as possible, as if you were working on the customer. Repeat the exercises for an hour.

STEP 1 STEP 2

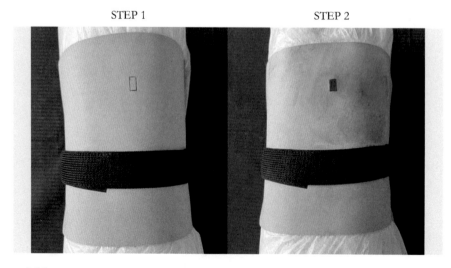

Filling

Lesson 3

Filling a rectangle with a MG

- **Step 1**

Take artificial skin and place it over a kitchen roll or similar. This simulates the curve of an arm or leg. Artificial skin must always be cleaned beforehand so that the stencil lifts. Draw a square measuring approx. 2.0 x 2.0 cm on the artificial skin with a pen. Now apply vaseline to the area to be tattooed and engrave the outlines.

- **Step 2**

Fill the area with the tip in place and use an 11 mm Magnum ø 0.35 needle. Make sure that the heel of your hand is always in contact with the surface. The artificial skin must remain on the table above the kitchen roll and must not be turned to suit your needs. Simulate stretching the skin on the artificial skin with your hand. Always practice as realistically as possible, as if you were working on the customer. Repeat the practice for one hour.

STEP 1   STEP 2

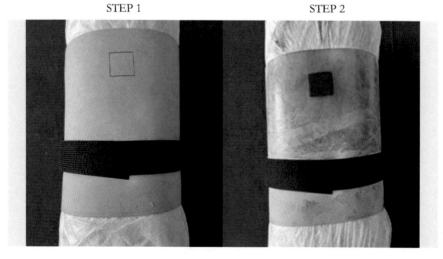

Filling

Lesson 4

Filling a rectangle with a SEM

- **Step 1**

Take artificial skin and place it over a kitchen roll or similar. This simulates the curve of an arm or leg. Artificial skin must always be cleaned beforehand so that the stencil lifts. Draw a square measuring approx. 2.0 x 2.0 cm on the artificial skin with a pen. Now apply vaseline to the area to be tattooed and engrave the outlines.

- **Step 2**

Fill the area with the tip in place and use an 11-gauge SEM ø 0.35 needle. Make sure that the heel of your hand is always in contact with the surface. The artificial skin must remain on the table above the kitchen roll and must not be turned to suit your needs. Simulate stretching the skin on the artificial skin with your hand. Always practice as realistically as possible, as if you were working on the customer. Repeat the practice for one hour.

STEP 1   STEP 2

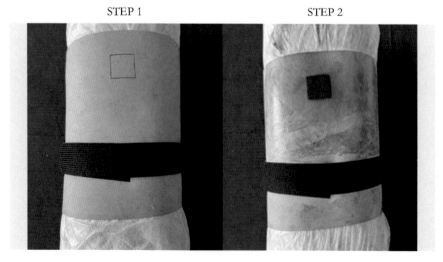

Filling

Lesson 5

Filling a star with a MG

▪ Step 1

Take artificial skin and place it over a kitchen roll or similar. This simulates the curve of an arm or leg. Artificial skin must always be cleaned beforehand so that the stencil lifts. Create a star motif on stencil paper and apply it to the artificial skin and wait approx. 20 minutes until the stencil is dry. Only then should you start tattooing. The stencil does not lift as well on artificial skin as it does on human skin.

▪ Step 2

Now apply vaseline to the area to be tattooed and engrave the outlines.

▪ Step 3

Fill the area with the tip in place and use an 11 mm Magnum ø 0.35 needle. Make sure that the heel of your hand is always in contact with the surface. The artificial skin must remain on the table above the kitchen roll and must not be turned to suit your needs. Simulate stretching the skin on the artificial skin with your hand. Always practice as realistically as possible, as if you were working on the customer. Repeat the practice for one hour.

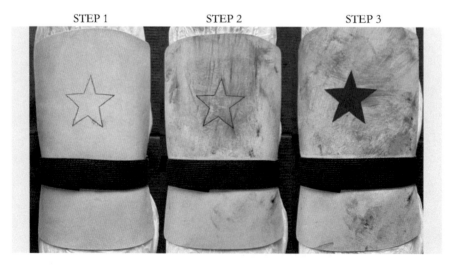

STEP 1   STEP 2   STEP 3

Filling

Lesson 6

Filling areas with red paint

- **Step 1**

Take artificial skin and place it over a kitchen roll or similar. This simulates the curve of an arm or leg. Artificial skin must always be cleaned beforehand so that the stencil lifts. Create a star motif on stencil paper and apply it to the artificial skin. Wait approx. 20 minutes until the stencil is dry and only then start tattooing. The stencil does not lift as well on artificial skin as it does on human skin.

- **Step 2**

Now apply Vaseline to the area to be tattooed and engrave the outlines of your motif.

- **Step 3**

Fill the areas with red paint and with the tip in place, using different needle types such as SEM, MG or RS. Make sure that the ball of your hand always rests on the surface. The artificial skin must remain on the table above the kitchen roll and must not be turned to suit your needs. Simulate stretching the skin on the artificial skin with your hand. Always practice as realistically as possible, as if you were working on a customer. Repeat the practice for an hour.

STEP 1   STEP 2   STEP 3

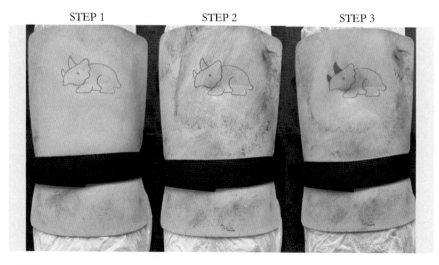

           Filling

Lesson 7

Filling surfaces in different colors

- **Step 1**

Take artificial skin and place it over a kitchen roll or similar. This simulates the curve of an arm or leg. Artificial skin must always be cleaned beforehand so that the stencil lifts. Create a star motif on stencil paper and apply it to the artificial skin. Wait approx. 20 minutes until the stencil is dry and only then start tattooing. The stencil does not lift as well on artificial skin as it does on human skin.

- **Step 2**

Now apply Vaseline to the area to be tattooed and engrave the outlines of your motif.

- **Step 3**

Fill the areas with red paint and with the tip in place, using different needle types such as SEM, MG or RS. Make sure that the ball of your hand always rests on the surface. The artificial skin must remain on the table above the kitchen roll and must not be turned to suit your needs. Simulate stretching the skin on the artificial skin with your hand. Always practice as realistically as possible, as if you were working on a customer. Repeat the practice for an hour.

STEP 1   STEP 2   STEP 3

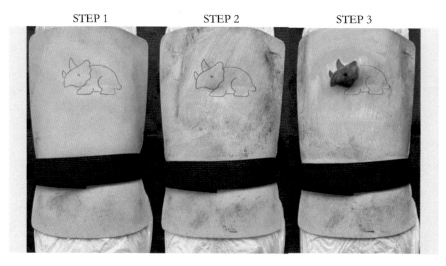

Filling

Shading

Soft shading is a quality feature of tattooing. For a tattoo to appear realistic, vivid and three-dimensional, the lines must be transformed into a shaded image. This means that the shadow of a motif must be tattooed. While the line mainly describes the contour, the shadows provide the viewer with information about the real shape of the motif.

The direction from which the light is coming is of great importance for the shape of the shadow. For a basic understanding of shadows, it is first important to know how shadows are created and what types of shadows there are. Shadows can only be created by light. They are created where there is little, hardly any or no light at all. The parts of a body that are completely facing the light source are also completely illuminated. If less light reaches an area because it is facing away from the light source or is obscured by another object, a shadow is created there. The less light reaches a spot, the more pronounced and therefore darker the shadow will be. Artists distinguish between body shadows (also known as inherent shadows) and cast shadows (also known as external shadows).

SHADING

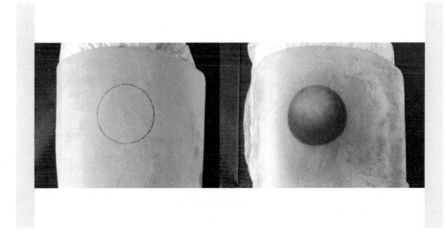

Shading

▪ 1. Cast shadow

Cast shadows are shadows that a body casts on the ground. They also provide the viewer with information about the shape of a motif, but more indirectly than body shadows. However, cast shadows best illustrate which side the light is coming from and at what angle it is falling.

▪ 2. light

The light in our surroundings ensures that we can see things around us with our eyes. Dark and light areas in a tattoo, which are created by the incidence of light, also lend a sense of realism.

▪ 3. body shadows

Body shadows are the shadows that a body creates on its own surface. They best describe the three-dimensional shape of the body.

SHADING

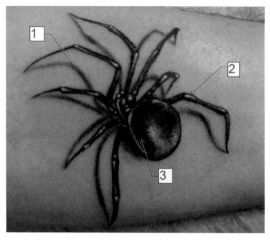

Shading

- **Tattooing shadows**

If you keep your design in mind when tattooing, shadows can become clear through good observation. Look at your motif and analyze the shadows that are created. You also need to determine how dark a shadow is. This is not easy, but plays an important role in the realistic and authentic effect of a tattoo. When tattooing the shadows, you must therefore work very carefully. Make sure that you do not shade too darkly. Areas that are too light can easily be darkened, but areas that are too dark can no longer be lightened.

- **Machine angle**

When shading, I work at an angle of 40-50 degrees to the skin.

NEEDLE ANGLE

Shading

- **Needle protrusion when working in place**

As with filling, the machine is held like a pen between the thumb and index finger, with the ball of the tattooing hand resting on it at all times. The hand should remain as flexible as possible. When shading, I tattoo with the tip in place with a needle protrusion of 0.9-1.5 millimeters. When shading, proceed in the same way as when filling. First the dark tones, then the light ones, as otherwise the colors can blend into the open pores. From my experience, I can say that the best shading is achieved with the Soft Edge Magnum. I also always try to work with the largest possible needle groupings, as the transitions between the shades are much smoother and more even. The following techniques are suitable for tattooing shadows:

NEEDLE STAND

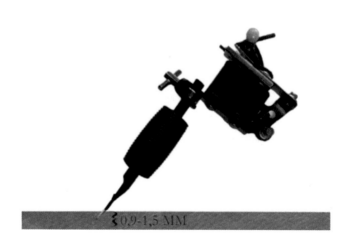

0,9-1,5 MM

Shading

- **Semi-pendulum shading**

In semi-pendulum shading, the needle is moved in front of the hand and gently lifted out of the skin at the end of the movement, as if you were sweeping with a broom. As a rule, the needle is pushed from the area that is to be darkest to the area that is to be lightest. Lifting the needle at the end of the movement makes the color gradient lighter there.

- **Pendulum Shading**

With pendulum shading, the needle is swung back and forth on the skin and gently lifted out of the skin at each point. By lifting the needle out at the end of the movements, the color gradient is lighter on the outside than in the middle.

SEMI-PENDULUM SHADING   PENDULUM SHADING

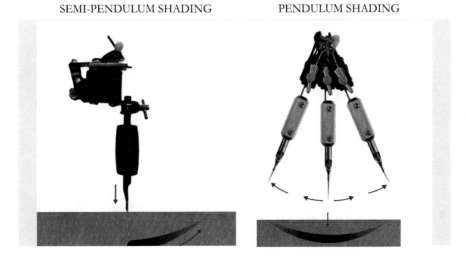

Shading

- **Whipe Shading / Pepper Shading**

Whipe shading is a technique for creating grainy shading. A low voltage is selected - around 5 volts depending on the tattoo machine. The needles are pushed in one direction with quick hand movements, causing the needles to bounce over the skin at increasingly larger intervals, resulting in a dotted gradient from dark to light.

WHIPE SHADING

Shading

▪ Pointillism / Dotwork

In pointillism, black dots are strung together to form shapes and lines. This style is particularly suitable for detailed patterns, ornaments and mandalas. The art here lies in lining up the dots correctly. The regular spacing of the dots is therefore most important, because if the spacing is too small, the dots will blur into one another over the years. Each dot must be placed in the correct position, as even the smallest deviations are immediately noticeable. A great deal of precision and patience is therefore required. In the field of shading, this is a very special method and brings realism to life in a very unique way. Amazing shading is possible, but it is usually limited as the dots are deliberately in the foreground. The individual dots replace the colors of other tattoos in this style, creating depth and realism. Therefore, the colors black and grey, rarely red, are used to achieve the unique effect. In this technique, I work with a flying needle and approx. 8 volts, depending on the machine.

POINTILLISM

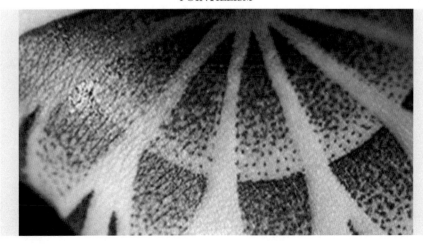

Shading

▪ Training plan for shading

In this training plan, you will practise various shading techniques and stretching the skin, among other things. Carefully consider and implement all the skills you have learned in the previous chapters in the training plan. If you are unsure about something, read the relevant chapter again. Practice continuously for an hour a day and you will make rapid progress.

Learning is like rowing against the stream. As soon as you stop, you drift back."
– Benjamin Britten

Lesson 1

Shade a small square with a RS

- **Step 1**

Take artificial skin and place it over a kitchen roll or similar. This simulates the curve of an arm or leg. Artificial skin must always be cleaned beforehand so that the stencil lifts. Draw a small square measuring approx. 1.0 x 1.0 cm on the artificial skin with a pen. Now apply Vaseline to the area to be tattooed and engrave the outlines.

- **Step 2**

Now shade the area with the tip in place and use a size 13 RS ø 0.35 needle. Make sure that the heel of your hand is always on top. The artificial skin must remain on the table above the kitchen roll and must not be turned to suit your needs. Simulate stretching the skin on the artificial skin with your hand. Always practice as realistically as possible, as if you were working on the customer. Repeat the practice for one hour.

STEP 1   STEP 2

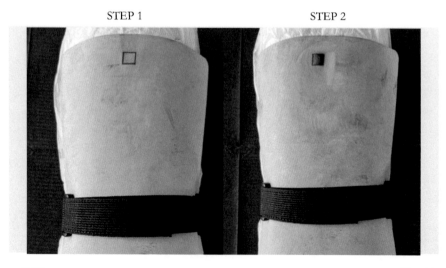

Shading

Lesson 2

Shade a square with a MG

- **Step 1**

Take artificial skin and place it over a kitchen roll or similar. This simulates the curve of an arm or leg. Artificial skin must always be cleaned beforehand so that the stencil lifts. Draw a square measuring approx. 2.0 x 2.0 cm on the artificial skin with a pen. Now apply Vaseline to the area to be tattooed and engrave the outlines.

- **Step 2**

Now shade the area with the tip in place from the right outer edge inwards using a 13 Magnum ø 0.35 needle. Make sure that the heel of your hand is always on top. The artificial skin must remain on the table above the kitchen roll and must not be turned according to your needs. Simulate stretching the skin on the artificial skin with your hand. Always practice as realistically as possible, as if you were working.

STEP 1   STEP 2

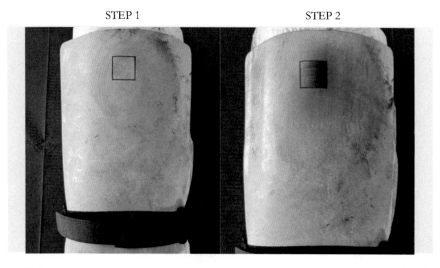

Shading

Lesson 3

Shade
a square
with a SEM

- **Step 1**

Take artificial skin and place it over a kitchen roll or similar. This simulates the curve of an arm or leg. Artificial skin must always be cleaned beforehand so that the stencil lifts. Draw a square measuring approx. 2.0 x 2.0 cm on the artificial skin with a pen. Now apply Vaseline to the area to be tattooed and engrave the outlines.

- **Step 2**

Now shade the area with the tip in place from the right outer edge inwards using a 13 mm SEM ø 0.35 needle. Make sure that the heel of your hand is always on top. The artificial skin must remain on the table above the kitchen roll and must not be turned to suit your needs. Simulate stretching the skin on the artificial skin with your hand. Always practice as realistically as possible, as if you were working on the customer. Repeat the practice for an hour.

STEP 1 STEP 2

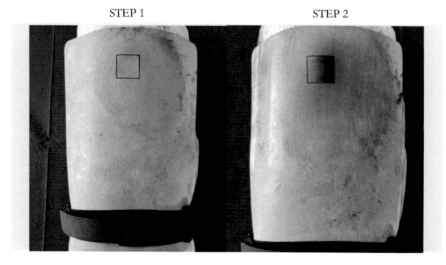

Shading

Lesson 4

Shade a circle with a SEM

▪ **Step 1**

Take artificial skin and place it over a kitchen roll or similar. This simulates the curve of an arm or leg. Artificial skin must always be cleaned beforehand so that the stencil lifts. Use a circle template to draw a circle with a diameter of approx. 4.0 cm on the artificial skin. Now apply Vaseline to the area to be tattooed and engrave the outlines.

▪ **Step 2**

Now shade the circle with the tip in place using a 13 mm SEM ø 0.35 needle. Make sure that the heel of your hand is always on top. The artificial skin must remain on the table above the kitchen roll and must not be turned to suit your needs. Simulate stretching the skin on the artificial skin with your hand. Always practice as realistically as possible, as if you were working on the customer. Repeat the practice for one hour.

STEP 1   STEP 2

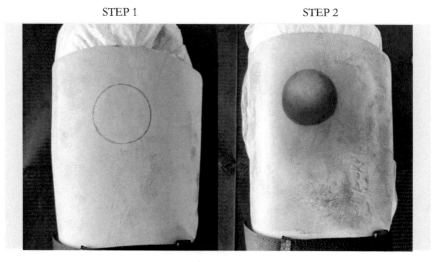

Shading

Lesson 5

Shade a star with a SEM

- **Step 1**

Take artificial skin and place it over a kitchen roll or similar. This simulates the curve of an arm or leg. Artificial skin must always be cleaned beforehand so that the stencil lifts. Transfer one of approx. 4.0 x 4.0 cm onto the artificial skin. Now apply Vaseline to the area to be tattooed and engrave the outlines.

- **Step 2**

Now shade the inner surfaces of the star with the tip in place so that the star is darker on the outside than on the inside, using a 13 mm SEM ø 0.35 needle. Make sure that the heel of your hand is always on top. The artificial skin must remain on the table above the kitchen roll and must not be twisted to suit your needs. Simulate stretching the skin on the artificial skin with your hand. Always practice as realistically as possible, as if you were working on a customer. Repeat the practice for one hour.

STEP 1 STEP 2

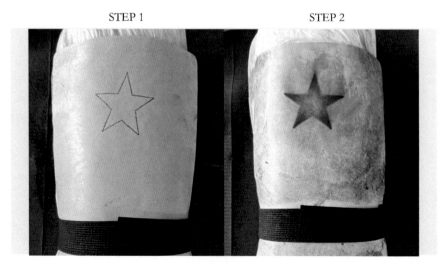

Shading

Lesson 6

Shade a star with a MG

- **Step 1**

Take artificial skin and place it over a kitchen roll or similar. This simulates the curve of an arm or leg. Artificial skin must always be cleaned beforehand so that the stencil lifts. Transfer a star measuring approx. 4.0 x 4.0 cm onto the artificial skin. Now apply Vaseline to the area to be tattooed and engrave the outlines.

- **Step 2**

Now shade the outer surfaces of the star with the tip in place, using a 13 Magnum ø 0.35 needle. Make sure that you become lighter towards the outside. The heel of your hand must always be in contact. The artificial skin must remain on the table above the kitchen roll and must not be turned to suit your needs. Simulate stretching the skin on the artificial skin with your hand. Always practice as realistically as possible, as if you were working on the customer. Repeat the practice for one hour.

STEP 1   STEP 2

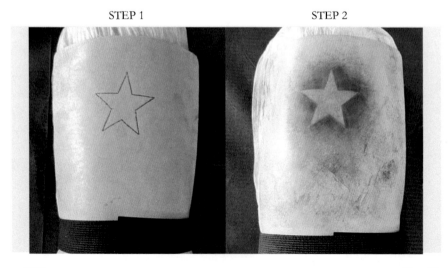

Shading

Lesson 7

Shade a motif with different needles

STEP 1 STEP 2

- **Step 1**

Take artificial skin and place it over a kitchen roll or similar. This simulates the curve of an arm or leg. Artificial skin must always be cleaned beforehand so that the stencil lifts. Create a motif on stencil paper and apply it to the artificial skin. Wait approx. 20 minutes until the stencil is dry and only then start tattooing. The stencil does not lift as well on artificial skin as it does on human skin. Now apply Vaseline to the area to be tattooed and engrave the outlines.

- **Step 2**

Now shade all areas using different needles. Make sure that the heel of your hand is always resting on the surface. The artificial skin must remain on the table above the kitchen roll and must not be turned according to your needs. Simulate stretching the skin on the artificial skin with your hand. Always practice as realistically as possible, as if you were working on a customer. Repeat the practice for one hour.

Conclusion

This book provides you with all the basics you need to become a professional tattoo artist. However, simply reading the book is not enough - it is important to understand the content and, above all, to practise a lot. If problems arise, check whether you are applying and implementing the techniques you have learned correctly. An inadequate approach or failure to observe the basics you have learned will already lead to inadequate results. In order to gradually increase your self-confidence as a tattooing novice, you should only engrave small, simple motifs and not on areas of the body that are difficult to engrave, such as the belly. Otherwise you may quickly become overwhelmed and lose interest in tattooing. Always remember that a tattoo is not a race, always take enough time, the speed will gradually come naturally. In the end, the only thing that counts is the result. So always be patient. You will also find that every tattoo artist uses different approaches and techniques - find out which method is best for you.

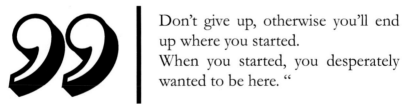 Don't give up, otherwise you'll end up where you started.
When you started, you desperately wanted to be here. "

"Good books don't end with the last page, they follow you for a lifetime!"

INKFESTAS

Tattoo Academy

Made in the USA
Las Vegas, NV
22 January 2024

84733223R00138